# TESTIMONIALS

These people know about the results that JoAn Majors and her speaking, training and coaching can bring to business and life. Whether you are an educator, entertainer, banker, attorney, CPA, medical/dental provider, team member or domestic engineer, read these words and then this book to become more significant to all those you encounter in life, business and your future!

Every time I speak with JoAn I learn something new—few people in life can affect others in this way. JoAn has a unique way of viewing the world. I mean sometimes it seems as if we're looking at the same scene through the same window, but JoAn sees the picture in a way none of us had. *EncourageMentors* does just that! JoAn cuts through clutter with incisiveness and commonsense rationale.

—**P. Christopher Holden**, President, Heraeus Kulzer, LLC

Using anecdote and Southern charm, JoAn Majors has written the handbook on how to encourage the folks you work with, live with and live for. She draws the human dimension out of both sides of the equation— parent and child, teacher and student, leader and team—and offers a perspective that integrates both. It's a most refreshing look at the steps to take in developing an open mind and a forgiving heart.

—**Linda Nyberg**, thirty-year high school business educator

Several years ago I debated upon traveling halfway across the country with my entire team to listen to a lady named JoAn Majors for I didn't know how it could possibly be worth the money I was about to put out. Today, whatever that amount was, it is the best investment I have EVER made. There are words that I use to summarize JoAn, not paragraphs; these words speak volumes about her: honesty, integrity and real. I am proud to call her my colleague, my partner and my friend. Just read this book. It's worth your time.

> —**Justin Moody**, DDS, DICOI; Founder of The Dental Implant Centers; Diplomate, American Board of Oral Implantology

*EncourageMentors* knocked me out! It's not just JoAn's practical nuts-&-bolts steps to take right now for a more encouraged life, it's the sense of humor and the womanly wisdom in the telling, the kind of book to read and re-read every few years.

> —**Claire Daly**, award winning baritone saxophonist, ClaireDalyMusic.
> com

JoAn Majors champions ideas for building businesses that take us out of short-sighted greed and into the judiciousness of the longer view. By encouraging compassion and cooperation among fellow workers instead of aggression and competition, she offers us a new understanding on how we do business and why significance is the better part of success.

> —**Jeff Chapman**, entrepreneur and business owner

*EncourageMentors* isn't just a book. It's who JoAn Majors is and what she truly does. To read the book is to see the real JoAn come to life on the page in all her spunky wit, business savvy, and inspirational style rolled into one.

> —**Danise Johnson**, Vice President, Prosperity Bank

The amazing JoAn Majors is a consummate professional, never leaving a stone unturned with her inspirational and motivational teachings. She speaks of guidance, and for certain, guidance is what she offers and what she herself received in abundance. At the core of her being is the word trust, trust in the good of all, trust in good business, trust in each and every person she mentors and guides. JoAn calls herself an "ardent student" of the virtues contained in this great literary guide on life, but indeed she plays both roles - student and teacher. She is truly a model of decorum and grace and "contagious care." It will forever be known that JoAn Majors didn't just learn the true meaning of life, she embodied it and courageously shared it with thousands. This very heartfelt and deeply personal diary is a lesson in life for us all. Thank you, JoAn, for sharing your truth with us.

—**Ana Ginja Quillinan**, marketing strategist
and Co-Founder, AMTM Consulting, LLC

After reading half way through JoAn's book, I called her and said I love it! The stories are heart felt and you feel like you are there experiencing them for the first time with her. Each step you can take and apply to an area in your life to help you become significant. As a 1st year teacher, I had a wonderful mentor guide me through one of the hardest but most rewarding years that I will never forget. This book does just that, it shows you what you need to look for in a mentor who will become a life long cheerleader for you!

—**Lindi Jurena**, second year educator

Think of a person who meant a great deal to you. Did she challenge you to be better? Did he push you to go past the limits you had set for yourself? Does that person still influence you today? Wouldn't you like to have that level of impact in the lives of others? JoAn Majors has provided an excellent handbook for becoming the mentor you want to be. *EncourageMentors* is a book that you can read quickly and will study for the remainder of your life. Learn its lessons and see your influence grow and flourish.

—**Randy G. Pennington**, author of *On My Honor, I Will:*
*The Journey to INTEGRITY-DRIVEN® Leadership*

Mentors matter! With joy I encourage you to the journey of mentorship by a master of words, methods and experience in the art of asking questions. Lived and written by a master-in-mentoring, JoAn Majors, the challenge is to significance, not just success.

—**Naomi Rhode**, CSP, CPAE Speaker Hall of Fame, Past President National Speakers Association, Past President Global Speakers Federation, Co-Founder SmartPractice

JoAn Majors has taken years of experience in customer service and sales to create the perfect handbook for encouraging success in business and life. I recommend this book to anyone who wants to see great results in business, families and the future. *EncourageMentors* is an indispensable guide to achieving your highest potential. This book is a must-read!

—**Pam Lontos**, President, PR/PR Public Relations, author of
*I See Your Name Everywhere: Leverage the Power*
*of the Media to Grow Your Fame, Wealth and Success*

This book is presented to

_____

in honor of

_____

From _____

On this date _____

# EncourageMENTORS

Sixteen Attitude Steps
for Building **YOUR**
Business, Family
and Future

# JoAn
# MAJORS

NEW YORK

# EncourageMENTORS

Sixteen Attitude Steps for Building **YOUR** Business, Family and Future

by JoAn Majors

© 2011 JoAn Majors. All rights reserved.

ISBN  978-1-60037-882-9  Paperback
ISBN  978-1-60037-883-6  EPub Version
Library of Congress Control Number:  2010939067

**Published by:**

**Morgan James Publishing**
The Entrepreneurial Publisher
5 Penn Plaza, 23rd Floor
New York City, New York 10001
(212) 655-5470 Office
(516) 908-4496 Fax
www.MorganJamesPublishing.com

**Cover Design by:**
Rachel Lopez
rachel@r2cdesign.com

**Interior Design by:**
Bonnie Bushman
bbushman@bresnan.net

For more information, contact JoAn Majors:
Write us at P. O. Box 880, Caldwell, TX 77836
Phone us at 1-866-51-CHOICE
Fax us at 979-567-9435
Visit our web sites: www.joanmajors.com

In an effort to support local communities, raise awareness and funds, Morgan James Publishing donates one percent of all book sales for the life of each book to Habitat for Humanity. Get involved today, visit
**www.HelpHabitatForHumanity.org.**

This book is dedicated to all the EncourageMentors whose work has only just begun and for those EncourageMentors in my life too numerous to mention here:

may you continue to find one and be one who inspires others to greatness!

# ACKNOWLEDGEMENTS

The people in my life who have been the closest to me started helping me with this book long before I ever conceived of writing it. Their contributions to my life and my work began back in a small town in East Texas where I grew up at 2116 Homewood Street. It was my formative years and their input is astounding to me as I now look back. Without friends and family who taught me and gave me spiritual guidance and discipline, I would never have known enough success as an encourager to justify writing this book in the first place. These pages owe a great deal to the teachings and writings of great business, motivational and professional development thinkers, both past and present, far too many to ever name adequately.

My thought is to begin a list of those closest in my circle of influence today, who have been there these last few years to encourage me during the loss of parents, a brother, dear friends, aunts, uncles and cousins alike. I remember that many of the items in this subject matter were a result of years of learning and those folks who I couldn't begin to locate today are equally entitled to a sincere thank you, wherever they are. Thank you to you all for your influence, however subtle or magnificent it was, and you know who you are!

Thanks to Kirpal Gordon of New York City whose translation of my Texas-Speak into written English is, as usual, a beautiful tribute to our language and its versatility. To the countless hours spent working out the details with my friend and confidant, Jeannie Russell. To Sandi Balcar for always making me feel like I just need to breathe and that overwhelm is a faraway place. For Pam Lontos whose inspiration, talent and opinions are mighty as well as her influence on this project. To Cyndi Zwernemann for letting me bounce ideas off her about what this book might look like, over and over.

To my family who amazes me with your support and tolerance of me when I am on a task like this one. Renee, Lou, Judy, Alfred, Donna and my late brother Gary for being in my life however, whenever you can. To our wonderful children, Kelli, Katy, Stacy and my son, JC, you will never know how your love completes me. Thank you for forgiving me for the missed ice hockey games, practices and family dinners while speaking or this manuscript took me away.

Last but certainly not least, my greatest EncourageMentor and the man without whom the title of this book would not have been born, my husband, Chuck. You cannot begin to comprehend how your steadfast love, support and belief in my abilities have built a great foundation for these words and all my work. It is my sincere hope that others will find a companion, friend, lover and life partner like mine. You are an amazing groom and my greatest champion!

To mom and dad, thank you for my life and your choice about me!

# TABLE OF CONTENTS

# PREFACE

*by Dave Weber*

JoAn Majors understands the dynamic power of the words we use. That's what has made her speaking presentations such a heart-moving and mind-opening experience. With her down-home humor, anecdotal style, infectious enthusiasm and refreshing authenticity, she has long embodied the intangible quality that causes us not only to see things anew but to act positively upon the wisdom she reveals.

Now she's written the book that does for readers what she has been doing for her seminar audiences for years: keeping it real, laughing while we're learning, challenging our pre-conceptions, delivering a truer understanding of our basic relationships at home as well as at work and inspiring us to choose a more service-oriented and generosity-driven lifestyle.

In addition, her new book could not be timelier for the sixteen attitude steps that constitute an EncourageMentor are the antidote for what's ailing our country. The recent financial meltdown, mortgage crisis, unemployment and recession that have undermined so many of us are the result of broken promises, insidious greed and fraud. JoAn, no stranger to adversity, maps out a step-by-step path away from such turmoil and returns us to the can-do mindset that has made us a great nation.

I dare you to read the first attitude step and see what I mean. I guarantee you that you'll find yourself way more encouraged than you were before.

# INTRODUCTION

If your life is going great guns right now, please don't read this book. If work and home life is all you ever dreamed of and everything's coming up roses, put this book back on the shelf and get one on investing or philanthropy.

Let someone else find this book, someone who has experienced discouragement, who knows it's not about him or her but who needs to know that giving up is not an option, someone who suspects care is contagious and that right can also be dead wrong, someone willing to take the high road if he or she could only find one, someone ready to go from nice and naïve to nice and knowledgeable, someone seeking to manage their own morale and willing to expose the elephant in the room. In short, this book is looking for someone ready to take at least a few of the sixteen attitude steps to a more encouraged outlook.

For those who want to open the door to new opportunities in a time when it seems that there are few, read on at your own quest.

1

## Attitude Step 1

# EVERYONE IS INCLUDED IN THE SEARCH FOR ENCOURAGEMENT

E veryone you meet is a candidate to become your mentor of encouragement. By that term I mean a trusted person who, by demonstrating heartfelt concern, focused attention, non-judgmental listening and sincere support, can help guide your way. Conversely, everyone you meet is also in search of an EncourageMentor, and regardless of your age, you hold the possibility of mentoring them through your life experience and expression of empathy, care, interest and confidence.

Encouragement may strike you as something a little lightweight, but these sixteen steps to a more encouraged attitude are, like Bette Davis said about growing old, not for the faint-hearted. To produce courage in another requires that your own life be the example.

That's a tough assignment, especially now. We live in an era of American history shaped by a sense of discouragement so enormous that it is holding us hostage and paralyzing our forward progress. The core values that have made us a great nation—our ingenuity, hard work, perseverance and concern for one another as fellow citizens—are threatened by a toxic combination of greed, fraud, incompetence and exploitation. The result for all strata of our society is a condition of imbalance, mistrust, uncertainty and cynicism. Hence, what rises to the surface is not our

American can-do-ness but rather our deepest, craziest fear (False Evidence Appearing Real).

Many people close to me have found themselves in such a downward, debilitating and unpredictable spiral. My brother-in-law Frank, a dedicated and responsible oil and gas worker in Wyoming, was placed on light duty and bullied into an undesired surgery not because of his performance but because of what was happening in the Gulf of Mexico. My sister Lou, who has grown better and better over the thirty-five years she has been in patient services, was downsized without fair compensation because someone higher up on the food chain couldn't balance the company's needs with its bottom line or face his own shortcomings as a manager.

Friends and associates who had been enjoying long and successful careers in business, education, media, law and service industries have shared similar tales of misfortune. The road these productive and valuable workers, from executive to janitor, have traveled has gone from being happily on the bus with a great seat to getting pushed off the bus before getting thrown viciously under the bus.

The loss of jobs is part of a larger story. Too many have lost hope to botched medical procedures, lost homes to mortgage scams, lost limbs to enemies on foreign soil, lost pensions to pyramid schemes, lost marriages to bankruptcy, lost loved ones to suicides and lost the children's college funds to financial pirates.

What I have found is that, although the challenges we experience in building our careers, businesses, families and futures are unique to us as individuals, we all need mentors of encouragement. How do I know? I get the visits, letters, phone calls and emails of the discouraged all the time. They get in contact with me because they are aware that I have perennially faced challenges in my personal and professional life, have learned from these life lessons and have grown a big encouragement tool box.

Although these lessons began early on, it wasn't until I lost my greatest EncourageMentor that I began to put the pieces together. Her name was Cecilia (Judy) Longoria Pickett and she was simply unstoppable, the epitome of an open mind and a forgiving heart. Born in a small town in south Texas, the daughter of a Mexican mother and a Spanish father, she was raised on a very poor farm. At age eleven she witnessed the accidental death of her father who was thrown off his horse and dragged by the reins. Being the oldest child, she quit school to go to work in the cotton fields and helped raise her brothers and sisters.

As a way out she married early in life and started a family. Her husband was, in her own words, "a nice man until he drank." His kind and loving Dr. Jekyll nature turned violent and Mr. Hyde cruel when inebriated. To put it diplomatically, his tormented world was a war between the good and evil within him, and with one small child in her care and another on the way, Cecilia feared that the next time he raised his hand to her might be her last. She found the courage to leave him and escaped with her children to another town.

However, only a short time later she met another man, equally good-natured when sober but equally abusive when drunk. One night, after suffering a particularly close call, she climbed out of a window with her children and started over once more. She returned to school and worked two jobs while she took care of her children. Another woman might have given up on marriage and men, but she kept an open mind and a forgiving heart. She soon met, fell in love with and married Earl Edward (Pete) Pickett, a man equally in love with her and amazed by her will to live. She had filtered out men with troubled souls and found a man inspired by her independent spirit and joy of life.

Initially issues arose for this white man's family regarding the choice of his bride and the color of her skin. It was an era marked by racist remarks, hostile attitudes and oppressive behavior. Another couple might have lost their wits or their loved ones, but they kept an open mind and a forgiving heart. With their first child together (now a blended family of five), they decided to live in the big city of Houston and launch a new beginning.

Challenges, however, struck Cecilia again, this time from a brain aneurism causing a major stroke at the age of only twenty-nine with their new child but a few months old. Told she would never walk, talk, write or speak again, she turned to her greatest EncourageMentor, her husband Pete. With his unflagging support she amazed her doctors daily with her charisma and tenacity throughout her year of physical therapy. Against all odds she was able to correct her paralyzed body and soon moved with a walker and finally just a limp, her right side now only partially paralyzed.

Another patient might have called it a day after such a victory, but defying the prognosis, she learned to write with her left hand and then she learned to speak again. Though the words came out in clipped bits of English and Spanish, her spirit was far from broken. Told she could not have any more children, she nevertheless discovered she was pregnant again. The doctors strongly advocated for the termination of the pregnancy as they foresaw challenges with this child, if delivered.

Well, that child is me. Although my husband and family will agree that I can be quite a challenge, none of these challenges are due to my mother's medical condition. I was born a very healthy baby, and being the youngest of seven children, I was cared for by most every member of the family.

I may have been the apple of my father's eye, but my dad Pete was well loved by all of mom's children. He paid off every medical bill we ever had with no assistance from anyone but his own hard work. He took care of us all despite being self-employed with no pension, profit sharing or disability income. An outdoorsman who loved to hunt and fish, he was not formally educated but he built a successful chemical and exterminating business as we shared a small two-bedroom, one bath home in East Texas. He also built something of great emotional wealth with my mother. They both had open minds and forgiving hearts—that's what they loved about each other, why neither tried to change the other and perhaps why us children felt so well loved.

One of my earliest memories is of walking with my mother and sister down a street in this small town. A local policeman heard my mom's broken speech and determined that she was an illegal Mexican. She was obviously handicapped and partially paralyzed but he didn't see it that way. He questioned her, and in spite of all we tried to say, arrested her, put her in handcuffs and took her and my sister and me to the county jail. Though he seemed intent on humiliating my mother, she was beyond his small-mindedness and maintained her dignity throughout the ordeal.

It was my first lesson in how to live with courage under duress. Finally given her one phone call, she rang dad who drove over to the jail to pick us up. At the appearance of her white husband, the arresting officer was visibly ashamed by the mistake he had made, and we were quickly escorted out. I remember the knowing and amused smile that my mother greeted my father with for it was stronger than any words either one of them might have said. These two EncourageMentors waited until we got home before they burst into laughter and tears at the injustice she had endured.

Mother was one of those people who struggled with health issues all her life but never complained, took pity on herself or suggested she ranked in a needier or more deserving position than anyone else. She battled breast cancer eighteen years apart. Back then they removed your breast down to the bone and offered nothing but a prosthesis that fit into your bra. She had heart stints, back surgery and a knee replacement on the "good leg" as she used to say. I remember a fall she'd taken getting out of the shower. Although she broke her coccyx bone, she didn't go to the doctor or let anyone figure it out for over a week. She just kept saying she'd be better tomorrow. She was finally taken to the hospital where she cried when someone assisted her in the things she prided herself on always doing on her own.

What struck all who met her—doctors, friends and neighbors—was her self-reliance. Alleged limitations did not limit her. She defied expectation and could not be reduced to the size of anyone's mind. No matter the degree of difficulty, she found a way. When we were in school she sewed our clothes, and I remember watching her bite the thread since using her right and left hand was a bit tough. The ponytails and pigtails my sister and I wore made us have tilted eyebrows because she would get it so tight with the grip of her teeth on one end of the rubber band. If that paralyzed right hand was opened enough to get a grip on something, it wasn't coming off easy.

I recall so vividly the day the pulmonologist brought us all together and told my mom about the spot he'd found on her recent chest x-ray. She looked at him with such hope and said, "Honey, me uh-need uh-get uh-little well so uh-cook and clean for Pete." As the doctor looked at us and then her, trying to tell her that she was in phase four cancer, his speech became broken, "You're not going to get better this time." She looked at him, wiped the tear from his eye and said, "Honey, you uh cry? Ugh ugh, me uh-live uh-good, uh-good life."

The last weeks of her life I spent as many hours as I could learning everything about her upbringing, her ordeals, her parents and yes, cooking Mexican food, too! Her life was the best "study" of an EncourageMentor I've ever had. I remember our last conversation was the day before my forty-third birthday. I was preparing to go back to my home when she patted the side of her bed and said, "Uh sit uh here, please." She shared in her broken words how she was so happy I had finally found my soul mate, a man who made me better in his presence and that she was proud that we were blessed with the birth of our child just a few years before. She ended by saying, "Honey, uh-please, uh-please, live uh-good, uh-happy life."

"I'll see you next week," I said, "you are being really silly," but she knew her time was ending and still sought to encourage me.

It was only later after she was buried awhile that I made sense of this for her death was like driving into an unfamiliar, unfriendly and uncomfortable fog. Not until I was on the other side of it and looked back in the rear view mirror did her presence in my life become clear. Because she was such a warrior of encouragement for me throughout my personal and professional life, I have come to understand the value of playing such a role in other people's lives. This remarkable woman with her miraculous story, beautiful smile and few words but with a heart as big as Texas is why I get up in front of thousands and speak about encouragement for this is not what I do—this is who I am.

The following fifteen attitude steps (chapters) are what she and my father lived and taught me by example. Rather than take false credit for attaining any kind of proficiency, I'm more disposed to sharing anecdotes that guide and inspire. I'm not the exemplar of these virtues, only their ardent student. Yes, onstage I am called "a powerhouse of enthusiasm" by audiences across the country, but I return to my home in a small Texas town where being a "professional woman" is considered an oxymoron. Instead of taking my supposed invisibility to heart or be limited by the blindness of others, I do the same as you would do: I volunteer my services to the community and mentor those who seek hope and encouragement.

Such people are everywhere, but you can't find them, as my parents so gently reminded me (over and over), until you open your mind, unclench your heart and include everyone in the search.

*JoAn's Parents–*
*45 years of Happy Marriage*

*JoAn's Mom and Dad*
*beginning their life together*

# Attitude Step 2

# NICE & NAÏVE TO NICE & KNOWLEDGEABLE IS THE JOURNEY

An open mind and a forgiving heart, one aware that everyone is your potential EncourageMentor or EncourageMentoree, tracks best with your detective instincts at work and in tact. After all, effective encouragement doesn't come from being nice and naïve; it comes from being nice and knowledgeable.

By nice I mean exemplifying courtesy. By knowledgeable I mean a hands-on, pro-active, in-the-trenches, learn-by-doing know-how forged from a mindset of continual improvement, not expertise in an academic area of study. The MBA is fine, but you want to become an MSH, one who Makes Stuff Happen.

That journey begins with a change in attitude about oneself. For some it involves heavy lifting, learning how to get one's head out of the sand and deliberately transforming a passive, done-to, woe-is-me point of view characterized by complaint, gossip and "It's not my fault" to one that is more people-friendly, results-driven, responsible for input and accountable for outcomes. For others, it's more like fine tuning, letting go of the prepared script of clichés and platitudes, paying closer attention to people and finding their deeper humanity. For many, it's about giving their natural curiosity a chance and retiring their inner Pollyanna, that

11

wide-eyed, overly optimistic character who wants to believe everything is wonderful even when it isn't.

Developing sound judgment and gaining maturity, insight and wisdom are all involved, but the acid test for losing the "nice and naïve" tag and graduating to the "nice and knowledgeable" accolade is your ability to focus on the fix, not the flaw. The fix is not just job-specific but an attitude about bringing your most responsive self to every situation.

It need not be a lifesaving event, but it could mean a lot all the same. For example, I was recently sitting with colleagues at a piano bar in the Orlando Hilton after a long day in seminar. The beverages were cold, the crowd was sparse, the ambience was just right, and the corner table we occupied seemed an ideal place to review the day's learning, at least until the piano man showed up a few minutes later. In no time at all, the volume of the music grew so loud that we could barely hear one another.

Sensing that something was wrong, Melissa, our accommodating young waitress, came to ask how we were doing. I inquired, "I know this is a piano bar, but isn't it a little too loud in here to talk?"

A true encourager, she smiled and said, "Just next door is David's Bar and Grill, a really quiet place at this hour, where I think you could have a great meeting. Would you like me to move your bar tab?" Her instinct was not to push back at my comment but to acknowledge my concern and focus on the fix.

Certain teachers do this naturally. In Jeannie's twenty-six years of teaching computer skills, web design and accounting to high school students, she never ran across a wrong answer she didn't want to know more about. By asking, "Will you show us how you arrived at that number?," she took the sting out of being incorrect, and while the student outlined his or her process step by step, the class helped discover where the wrong turn was made, strengthening their own competence in the material which motivated an eagerness to solve more complex problems. Because Jeannie knows that real learning is not just getting the right answer on a test but includes an engaged dialogue where minds meet, discussion ensues and solutions are found, her method demonstrates that it's not really a mistake unless you fail to learn from it.

An environment of encouragement, free of fear and put down, is not just the right answer, whatever the question, it's the cure. The joy of discovery becomes a communicable experience when everyone is focused on the next piece of the puzzle—everyone except the self-righteous and the nay-sayers. Immune to the contagion of discovery, they can't lose themselves in the group or in the search, and once something's broken, they can't fix it.

Put simply, they are obsessed not with discovering solutions but with who's right (me) and who's wrong (you) because that's what matters: being the hero of one's own narrative, not serving the common good. It is much easier to focus on the flaw and avoid any responsibility for the fix. It's like complaining there is a flaw in your town that won't allow people to appreciate successful professional females versus being "the change you want to see in the world," as Mahatma Gandhi phrased it, in this case moving toward a deeper appreciation of the unique worth of everyone in the town.

Any time I find myself casting shame or avoiding blame at the expense of others, I know I'm far from the fix. In spite of this obvious wrong direction, people of all persuasions, from the least literate to the most educated, do it all the time. I got a phone call from a friend who almost lost her life because the trusted specialist who treated her just could not be wrong. He said her bothersome tooth needed to be removed and replaced by a dental implant. She had no issue with his diagnosis, so he and his team removed the tooth and prepared the site for a bone graft and membrane that same day. However, upon returning home, she felt feverish and called to report a feeling of sickness that she felt was in direct relationship to the surgery. The doctor disagreed, and though he never offered to see her, he said she probably had an infection and that he would call in more antibiotics and she would be better soon.

All that week she grew more violently ill with a mounting fever and continuous sweats. She called again and was told in no uncertain terms, "It can't be anything we did." Meanwhile, a client of hers, an ER doctor, thought she could be going into septic shock and that she should seek immediate medical help. He said, "If you have something new in your body no one can really say, 'It can't be anything we did,' since all people are not the same and you could have a reaction that was unique and previously undocumented."

A trusted ENT friend of hers admitted her, and as a courtesy, called the dental specialist and suggested nicely (and knowledgeably) that something should be done. The specialist came to the emergency room and actually removed the membrane he had placed. Within two hours her fever dropped and her sweats subsided.

What was the specialist thinking? Not too much. Like many of us, he didn't want to be confused by the facts. In spite of his degrees and advanced training, his mind was made up before any evidence could arrive to disclaim it, so in spite of her condition he didn't need to see her. His need to be right could have been dead wrong for her, however, if not for the quick-thinking ENT and her ER doctor friend. Granted, her reaction to the treatment was highly unusual and extremely rare, but as her dentist, why would he not offer to take a look at the very least?

Having to be right isn't just arrogance. It's a disease that kills, and in order to fight back we must get to know it by its first symptom: a failure to consider the other's point of view. I'm a big fan of Steven Covey's work and I love his adage, "Seek first to understand then to be understood," and quote it often when I am working with a team or company whose members feel misunderstood. By giving the very thing you most want to get, you create the circumstance to be better understood. By stepping back to consider what the other side might be seeing, hearing, or feeling that is causing the problem, a curiosity is born, and when needing to know out-motivates needing to be right, a dialogue that gets down to the heart of the matter can begin.

This is what the nice and knowledgeable have discovered. To gain the courage to encourage, all they had to lose was their naïveté.

## Attitude Step 3

# CARE IS CONTAGIOUS

C aring for one another is not just good common sense or a virtue of leadership; it's a survival skill forged into our gene code. Attending to the concerns of those around you is a small, learnable virtue that delivers enormous results. By paying attention to others with one's own heart and head directly connected, we give our common humanity a little more of a chance.

Reaching out to those among us who are in need of concern helps put our better nature forward. It also inspires, encourages and invites others to express concern as well. We no doubt like to think of ourselves as individuals, but we're also a highly sociable species, far more interconnected than we realize, susceptible to a plethora of emotional cues, even ones we are not conscious of, and to engage one another altruistically is the least we can do. If a pleasant greeting is met with a petulant reply, the greeter's elated mood can be quickly deflated, and the opposite is just as true. I can't tell you how many times a very agreeable gesture has not only turned my gloomy day around but made me want to impart that good gesture to others.

So many of us dwell in a pre-existing condition of feeling unheard and unseen that just by paying attention we can be of assistance. Although we're only being called upon to care, not to solve problems and change lives, listening with one's heart can help end or mend that sense of isolation which can seem overwhelming.

It's also a reminder how contagious care can be. We're way more apt to show concern when others show concern. Some years ago I walked into the bathroom at Disney World where a very young mother was struggling to hold it together as her small, hot and sweaty daughter was throwing up in her stroller in the middle of the floor. While the two young boys with her danced around as if they were under blues skies, the mother was clearly at her wit's end, yet female after female offered no assistance. They looked away, stepped over the vomit and kept moving.

I have the same aversions to these sights and smells as anyone, but I could see things getting worse by my simply doing nothing. So I sprinted to the eating area and grabbed as many paper towels as I could carry. I apologized to the family I stepped in front of and said there was a young mom with an emergency in the bathroom. The lady who let me in line then followed behind me with more towels and a cleaning professional from the park.

As we moved the two boys out of the way and helped the mom clean the floor and disrobe her young daughter, I realized that where once women rushed to get out of the way, they now helped out however they could. Over the sink the young mom confided to me, "My husband isn't feeling well and I figured I could handle it. I mean a mom ought to be able to, right?"

"I always leave the house believing I can, too," I assured her, "but thankfully someone is around to help me when I need it—and I usually do need it!"

We laughed and she seemed visibly relieved. Then she thanked each of us as we went on our way.

In so many situations, it seems as if we're all waiting for a cue to respond with care instead of callousness. I really enjoy watching "What Would You

Do?," the TV program with John Quinones that features everyday people confronting a moral dilemma: an animal left in a hot car, an airplane pilot drinking and stumbling from the cocktail lounge to his flights, a gay couple with children being harassed by a homophobic waiter. I get caught up in the suspense of what makes people step up and do the right thing. In a recent episode a Downs syndrome actor played the role of a young man who was bagging groceries in a local store. While the mean person checking out (also a staged actor) insulted the bagger, calling him slow, odd and even retarded, many of the people in line or walking by made a face of outrage or a remark of disgust but very few intervened. However, those who did intervene, the true EncourageMentors, were interviewed about why they spoke up. Although they said that they sought to be respectful of other people's boundaries, they also sought to protect the bagger whose boundaries had been crossed by the mean shopper.

Their sense of justice overrode their sense of privacy. My son, now eleven, will often see someone with a hood open in a parking lot and say to me, "I know we have jumper cables so do you think we should go over and help?"

Because expressing concern for others is a modeled behavior, we don't really teach this value so much as model this value to our children. I know that for the value to have meaning for my children it must be congruent with my own heart and mind and consistent in my responses to others. So I want to be a person who models concern for others not just to my children but also in my professional life.

Fortunately, Jeannie, the encouraging high school teacher in Chapter 2 who never met a wrong answer she didn't want to know more about, is my ultimate team member. She is also someone who understands and models the same values I have. I was introduced to her by may husband who had met Jeannie in her prior work with the Texas Academy of General Dentistry, an organization of which he is a member of and was working toward a Mastership certification. It turned out that she lived near Austin some seventy-five miles from us and had met and fell in love with a neighbor and friend of ours. She was leaving the AGD and moving to our little community!

On first meeting her I felt a bit intimated since I knew she had worked with the booking and arrangements for many doctor speakers. I was going through some change as Beckey, my assistant for nearly seven years was going back to full-time work in an previous job. So I invited her to go to California to work with me on a two and one half day program I was offering. At the first break, she walked up to me and said, "You really are what I thought you were! You are living the message you deliver from the stage and I'd like to join forces." The rest, as they say, is history!

We struck a deal that we both liked, she gave her two week notice and came on board. Immediately, I began to see incredible results. Yes, it helped that she had worked with some professional speakers, but what really made things different was the bond of trust and care for clients that we forged. It is liberating to work with others for whom care is contagious.

Restaurant entrepreneur Anatole Iwanczuk, an immigrant from Ukraine who grew up on the streets of New York, knows how vital the interaction between his kitchen and dining room/bar can be for his Upper East Side establishment.

"One of my best servers, Frankie, asked me to give his brother Jim a job so I finally hired him," he told me, "though lackadaisical was the best way to describe the guy. The primary work of a busser is to clear tables and set up for the next guests, and if that goes slowly, the business goes slowly. Naturally, the other bussers resented Jim and felt they were carrying him. Out of concern for Frankie, I worked hard to give Jim the attention and guidance he needed. Although it took a while, he not only became my best busser but a caregiver in everything he did. Others on staff caught the bug and started helping out those they had thought of as slackers.

"It was an amazing turnaround, but of all the caring workers I've hired over the years, Roberto is the standout. He cared about my business as much as I did. An ordinary looking fellow, small but strong, he was from Mexico and spoke little English, but he was a very good listener. I hired him to do anything I needed, whether helping out with construction, playing go-fer or cleaning up. Initially I was slightly hesitant, not knowing whether I could fully trust him, but little by little, he won me over. By the time I opened the restaurant, Roberto was doing my bank runs. He gained a good deal of pride and confidence as I continued to increase his responsibilities. Everyone in my place knew that Roberto was 'the man,' but instead of puffing him up, it only made him more responsible. As his English improved, he worked with several of the kitchen help to improve theirs. He guided each new hire around and gave them extra attention while they were learning the ropes. Other employees on our team came to him with their problems and relied upon his listening skills and leadership. The quality of his care and concern had become contagious."

The value of caring for one's clients is now changing how many educators and health professionals view their job. In *A Whole New Mind, Why Right-Brainers Will Rule the Future*, Daniel H. Pink offers some surprising material on the curriculum changes in American medical schools. Students are being trained in what he calls "narrative medicine." It turns out that, despite advances in technology, much of the diagnosis is contained in the patient's story, something doctors and their teams are now taking a closer look at when making a diagnosis.

I predict that it won't be long until this client-centered approach spills over into the education curriculum of attorneys, accountants and finance industry players. I was apprised of a situation where a friend had sent her sister to an attorney for whom she had great respect, attended the same church with children the same age—in short, the perfect referral. However, the sister shared with me that the attorney did not listen to her. He never took a note on their first meeting and had to ask for her children's names three times.

As professionals, we must first acknowledge that there is a person attached to the illness, divorce, family death, tax statement or spreadsheet.

By expressing care and concern, we spread care and concern to those we hope to serve in a professional capacity.

# Attitude Step 4

# OPPORTUNITY COMES DISGUISED

In the midst of heartbreak, career uncertainty, family challenges or just the turmoil of hard times, have you ever sensed that hidden in such a *mess* lay your *mess*age, that your future depended upon your discovering opportunity within the adversity?

Some years ago I found myself in such a crisis, tangled up in ethical issues with the CEO of a seminar company I once had loved and admired. Having made his wealth in another industry he knew that for his training to be credible to dental teams he had to gather some of the best in the field to his company, and I was among the ones who felt honored to speak on his stage. It was a wild ride and when things took a turn for the worse, the dedicated professionals who had originated the seminar, people I looked up to for the depth of their commitment, were feeling less than encouraged.

The company was growing exponentially, but the numbers promised to them had not been delivered. When the conversation turned to his young partner who took his wallet out, pitched it on the table and said, "As for the seminar, I want you to part the plastic from their hips every time you get the chance this week-end," I swallowed hard. I couldn't forget that I'd served this industry for fifteen years and had never thought this way, nor could I forget that my husband was attending that seminar! It's funny because friends in the company lovingly referred to us as the poster couple for the dental program.

So how did I go from poster girl to pink slip?

I demanded that the CEO live in life the principles of honesty, fair play and integrity we espoused from the stage. Yowie, did I overstep a boundary! When he got in my face, jabbed his finger into my chest and told me to shut up, my heart broke. I had questioned authority and discovered that scruples mattered more than I ever thought. The price of admission was that my dream gig with this industry-leading seminar company was over.

I knew he couldn't teach me anything more and that meant I had to move on. As for his limitations with sharing the wealth, I understood that fear because my daddy was a Depression era baby, too. Holding tight purse strings was how one survived the time, but if left unchecked, the effect of that scarcity mentality is to see greed as good and stinginess as thrift. Through the love shared among us, we had outgrown that kind of fearful thinking as a family and now I saw that I had outgrown my opportunity with this company.

The pink slip knocked me down at the time, but after blaming myself in a thousand and one different ways, it became my personal permission statement to build my own company later, seek my own audience with my own message and walk my own talk. It took plenty of retrospection to see that the CEO had not just made it impossible for me to stay but that he opened a door that brightened my own future when I finally walked through it.

I had to forgive myself for placing ethical expectations upon him, expectations that I have since placed upon myself where they are a better fit and do me some good. Perhaps that's what he was telling me the whole time, I don't know. I do know, however, that dealing with that experience and finding a new frame of mind came in very handy a few years later.

At almost forty years of age, I was blessed with the birth of my own biological child. When I married my husband six years earlier, his three beautiful and amazing daughters from an earlier marriage really welcomed me into the fold. I didn't replace their mother, with whom I get along very well, so much as become their "bonus mom," a phrase that they still use to this day.

Like in the household in which I was raised, a blended family in which both my parents had children from previous marriages, we never used phrases like step-child or half-brother. Those words did not accurately describe us for we all felt fully related and glad to have one another, even more so when we started our own families.

So when my son was born, everyone in the family, including his three healthy and perfectly formed sisters, was overjoyed with the new addition. However, he was diagnosed with syndactaly, a birth defect that happens in the womb at about eight weeks. An amniotic band does not release and causes the malformation of a particular hand, arm or muscle. His condition required two surgeries to separate his fingers on his left hand before he was a year old.

A more enlightened mother would have been glad just to have a child, but I imagined that his condition was my fault. What had I done wrong? Somehow his birth defect was my punishment for something I'd done earlier in my life. Like with the pink slip, every day I invented new reasons to blame myself.

An encourager who knew what I was going through gave me an article (a daily devotional) that talked about how few parents are chosen to receive the gifted children, the ones who show us a world far beyond our own aspirations for our "perfect child." In short, I saw in my son's eyes what I saw beaming back to me from my mom and dad: the look of pure and unadulterated love. It was another chance to model a value and a behavior. Little did I know that it wouldn't be the last.

A month before his fourth birthday, my son traveled by life flight helicopter to Texas Children's Hospital in Austin. He had a serious, fast-acting respiratory condition. Although it happened too quickly for me to blame myself, this emergency mission opened a door into a larger understanding. In the ten days that we spent in Pedi-ICU, we witnessed six children under the age of six lose their lives to influenza. I saw what a blessing it was to have a child who was such a fighter for life just like my mom. In fact, one month after I lost my mother to cancer, he—a mere five and a half years old—was diagnosed with cancer.

This time we set off for Texas Children's Hospital in Houston in some shock and uncertainty, but once again he had a successful procedure and a complete recovery. The doctors who read the scans of the cancerous thyroid tumor prior and insisted on the full surgery described it on the day after as nothing more than fatty tissue. They might as well have said, "Nothing short of a miracle," because that's what it was to us.

An articulate young man now eleven years of age, he is a fierce and skilled ice hockey player as well as a baseball lover. He also plays basketball and soccer, likes to swim and loves to ride motocross. He recently said to me, "Mom, I'm gonna have a great testimony one day, aren't I?"

At that, I'll just say he already has.

However, my learning curve has proven slower than his. Whether grappling with career changes, my mother's death or my son's medical issues, please don't think I walked around feeling calm and wonderful, saying things like, "Oh, here we go again with another opportunity, what a treat and a blessing in disguise."

No, I crawled toward that conclusion after a ton of real stinkin' thinkin' that had me crying, "Why me, Lord?" and wearing out the Book of Job! In short, I freaked out in every possible way before I stumbled upon the blessing of the mess: give up trying to fit the occasion into your mind; instead, change your mind to better fit the occasion. The CEO wasn't firing me but sending me out in the world to find my own audience using my own moral compass. My son was in a life or death struggle, but like my mom, he kept showing me throughout his trials the other side of alleged disability: a warrior's will to live and a loving heart.

These were truths (and opportunities) I could not grasp at first, thanks to my self-induced pity party with huge doses of guilt, anxiety and distress in the mix. Having already traveled the length and breadth of that route, I know it's a dead-end. If this attitude step provides any relief from such foolishness to those seeking or giving encouragement, I'm glad to disclose my own foolishness and reveal what changed in my way of thinking that has so powerfully changed my life.

*JoAn's strapping son, JC,*
*before a hockey game*

# UNDERSTAND IT'S NOT ABOUT YOU

I grew up in East Texas among country folks who liked to turn a phrase, and as a child I remember asking my older sister Renee why adults said, "He came home and kicked the dog."

"Sometimes we lash out at others in anger or frustration. Kicking the dog means an earlier event set off the ugly behavior."

"So it means it's not about you?"

"You just happen to be where the tongue-whippin' took place."

"But what if you're at the mercy of the lashing?"

"It's still not about you. So don't get your feelings hurt or take the heat for solving the problem he or she is 'venting' about. It didn't have anything to do with the dog either."

I understood the phrase, but even as a child I wanted it to be about me; I wanted to be of service, to influence the outcome, to make it better. Years later, making it about me and helping solve the problem was all I knew how to do. It was the fuel I used to motivate myself to achieve and to become more responsible. I was sure that making it about me was making me a better daughter, sister, wife, mother, speaker, team leader, change agent and EncourageMentor.

However, as I alluded to in the previous attitude step, it wasn't until lives near and dear to me were on the line that I saw the harder, fuller truth. Making it about me hadn't exerted any actual influence on these crucial outcomes in any way whatsoever. When my mother and son became ill, in spite of all my skill training in communication and problem solving, I was cast into that most humble of human predicaments: watching from the sidelines, unable to help, reduced to tears. All I could do was pray. It was a tough way to learn that most of what happens is not about me, but I finally got the message—and just in time to re-learn the lesson in my professional life.

When my mother passed and my son got better, I struck out on my own as a speaker and trainer and was soon enjoying more revenue than I had ever expected. I accepted invitations to teach at premier training institutes, my reputation as "a team member who has temporarily left the office" was building and my first book hit the stands garnering high praise in my industry. I had found my voice and my niche audience, and my calendar was filling up with speaking engagements.

After reading (and re-reading) some particularly glowing reviews on the critique forms from my last seminar, I had a chance to sit down with my mentor, Naomi Rhode, a real lady who has had incredible success in the same industry. I told her the joy I felt in being so well received as a speaker but that something wasn't quite right, that I sensed I was missing something.

"You've tasted success, but have you experienced significance?"

Her words caught me by surprise. I took a breath and let the question sink in. What was I really teaching from the front of the stage—how to have success or how to have significance?—and what was I representing to my audience, my success or my significance?

I wanted to be significant but the more I thought about it, the more I realized that my need to succeed was making me insignificant. I was afraid of defeat, any defeat, even just the perception of defeat, and this resulted in my making some poor decisions during the seminar, like trying to bring along Mr. Arms Crossed, that guy in the back of the room who looked like he had his face soaked in pickle juice. Thanks to Naomi's distinction, I saw him for who he was: not an affront to my effectiveness or a challenge to my ego, but a conflicted learner who had his own deal going on—one that wasn't about me!

By making it about me I was actually blocking the path to my greater effectiveness. It would have been better to let him come and join us in his own time. Rather than reach out to the unreachable one and risk losing the attention of those I had already reached, his peers' urgent motivation would do far more to inflame his interest than anything I could ever do. It really wasn't about me—and that was a relief I was just beginning to enjoy.

Still, Naomi's question kept me up that night and forced me to confront the evidence that I was taking myself too seriously and losing my grasp on what really mattered. I had focused on teaching replicable systems of bottom-line success to teams, but the folks in my seminar also wanted assistance in their pursuit of significance. It was all there in the feedback they had written, but I'd been so intent on reading for confirmation I'd done well that I hadn't seen it. So I started to change my approach. I wanted to encourage my audience to find more meaning in what they did and to take action steps that made their lives, families and careers work in greater harmony. Now at the start of my every seminar I began to ask what Naomi asked me, "You've tasted success, but have you experienced significance?"

Reporting that the fastest way to feeling more significant as a professional, partner or parent was not to take everything personally, they shared tales of letting go of their own tendencies to control outcomes in favor of being more present and "letting the game come to you," as my son's hockey coach calls it. Story after story revealed that It's-not-about-you wasn't a self-serving act of irresponsibility but an attitude adjustment. Not only is there no need to push the river for it flows by itself, but if we knew how little folks cared about what we said or thought, we'd worry less what they'll say or think about us.

Through these testimonies of lightening up and letting go, we touched upon a deeper truth about how we learn, expressed in the phrase: "When the student is ready, the teacher will appear." This idea provided the remedy to worry and despair. Knowing that these things tend to take care of themselves, we saw that our job as seminar students was to create a condition of readiness.

There's always more learning, more wisdom and more laughter to be had when it's not about you.

# RIGHT CAN ALSO
# BE DEAD WRONG

It wasn't looking good for the lawyer on the witness stand. His client had apparently committed a heinous murder, beaten the rap and now may have murdered again. The district attorney, certain that he had the murderer's co-conspirator red-handed, smiled, paused, looked to the jury and asked the lawyer, "Did you not represent the client in question and find a way to have the police who did the investigation become the ones in question themselves?"

All eyes were on the lawyer. No doubt about it, he was going down.

"That is accurate," he stated calmly, "but not true. I had represented the client in question on the first charge, a trumped up case whose evidence was sloppily handled. As for the police who investigated, they were questioned due to their inabilities to connect my client to the crime, not because of my abilities as a lawyer to disconnect him."

Accurate but not true, that's so well said—and what a switcheroo, how the accusers became the accused. I love courtroom dramas and their dance of words. Every time someone answers a question, a whole new picture of events is likely to reveal itself. It's another reminder that perception is a question of perspective, that right can be dead wrong.

As Dave Weber shares this in his book, *Sticks & Stones Exposed: The Power of Our Words*, take the spots on a leopard's coat, for example. Five inches from the human eye, they appear to be nothing but a repeating pattern of squiggles in different sizes. However, five yards away from our eyes, a do-or-die, fight-flight response kicks in because it's clear that those spots belong to a stealthy predator.

It's all a question of scope.

Like the ghosts and goblins that live under the creaky floorboards in our darkened homes but are betrayed by day's first light, our fear-driven imaginations often have a lot to do with what we see. You might say that we are using our eyes not to absorb information but to edit out what doesn't fit our pre-existing picture of events. Like the dental specialist in Attitude Step Two who insisted he was Dr. Gotta B. Right and who almost made my friend Ms. Dead Wrong, not seeing reality can become a full time job with major consequences.

By projecting arrogance and infallibility, we only complicate matters, and when we are questioned about our performance and attack the questioner with a how-dare-you smugness, we are eliminating any hope of getting it right. We may think we have hidden our insecurities from others by accumulating status, wealth, advanced degrees and the images of success, but we are way better off admitting that we are only human and could be wrong.

If as professionals we cannot acknowledge that we err, how much humanity are we offering those who seek our care? The problem with de-NILE, as any Egyptian will tell you, is that it builds and builds and then floods out everything for miles. Likewise, the reflex to blame others only reveals our own shortcomings. By putting down team members for their ineptitude just so we might look better, we add to the perception of our own ineptitude a lack of loyalty and a failure to be responsible. If this is how the leader treats team members, it's a pretty good indicator that the customer won't be treated any better.

Although total disclosure solves the problem, we are reluctant to ask the right questions. It's not that we don't know what to ask; it's staring us in the face. It's that some answers, just like our decisions to care, require that we change, and it is a fear of change that keeps us silent.

Earlier in my life, I was married to a man for a short time with whom I shared an amazing number of things in common. We were both go-getters raised in small towns, we had parents who were still married, we enjoyed the same kinds of food and liked the same kinds of people, but most of all we both shared a love of the outdoors. Both of us grew up hunting, fishing and camping as a family.

I foresaw the years of bliss we would enjoy by doing these things together just like my loving mom and dad, but he foresaw our future with me understanding that I would be staying home while he went out hunting, fishing and camping with his buddies. Included or excluded? Our different definitions of togetherness killed the marriage we both thought would last a lifetime.

Suffice to say, I learned to ask more questions to prospective partners. I needed to make sure that we not only had values, love and affection in common, but that we had the same definitions for things like together and separate, male and female, work and play, homemaking and bringing home the bacon.

I got better at checking my own assumptions. I learned to give my curiosity a freer rein and ask more questions. Like any other skill, asking takes practice before it can become second nature. I expected that mistakes would be made and that developing a learning curve would be crucial. Like my mother's pursuit of a loving, sober partner and father for her children, a search that ended with her meeting my dad, I learned to filter out the whimpy complainers, the macho ego trippers and the delicate grand poobahs. I learned more about where the other person was coming from, improved my perception and gained a better perspective. By the time I met Chuck on a first date, I knew not only what to ask but what I was really looking for as well. It turned out that who and what I was looking for was also looking for me.

So much of human communication is an attempt to get the golden rule right, but doing unto others the way you would want them to do unto you can easily become misread. In order to be effective, the platinum rule works better: do unto others the way they want to be done unto, not the way you want to be done unto. In order to see more clearly who that other person really is, I have used an age-old tool for personality identification. It's called DiSC. Understanding our own character better with its likes, dislikes, strengths and weaknesses is something that makes coming home to my house a joy.

In my business I am a decision maker, team leader and mover of mountains! In his business, he is a no-nonsense detailed planner and predictable provider of care, skill and judgment with little or nothing left to chance.

In our personal lives I am a follower of my strong and determined husband. My robust, interactive personality loves the lengthy story and all the details whereas he often prefers the most abridged version. We have created a happy medium ground by giving each other permission to say things like this, "JoAn, I know the whole story is important to you, but I can't listen to it all right now. Would you like to give me the bottom line or wait until later when I have time to talk and listen?"

This would have committed me to tears years ago, but now it's easy and it works. I can say to Chuck, "I have a time constraint and need to know if you can pick JC up from the game" without making any more out of it, especially when time is limited. I've also grown more aware of what kind of day he may have had, and when I sense he's been challenged by something at work, I stick to few questions and plenty of big open space for him to find his own time to communicate what's on his mind.

I had to learn that my way of thinking may be the right way for me, but it can be dead wrong with him. We love other enough to communicate in the ways we each prefer and we each find time to listen to the stories that we need to share. It's the ultimate way of caring and sharing.

*JoAn and the love of her life, Chuck*

# ATTITUDE IS THE ONLY THING WE **CAN** CHANGE

In discouraging times, it can be hard to find courage, and we often turn to our heroes of legends. They do extraordinarily courageous things: they climb the highest mountains, descend the deepest depths of the underworld, fly through the sky, slay deadly dragons and calm the seven seas. Not only do their super-human actions change our calamitous course and restore the balance of heaven and earth, they encourage the hero in us to come out from hiding and dare us to deliver equally courageous acts.

Compared with leaping tall buildings in a single bound, the ability to change our attitude may not seem all that courageous or exciting, but it's where the real action is and it's all taking place right between our ears. A parable about attitude may help illustrate this.

A barefoot prince searches out his kingdom for a wise man living deep in the forest. When he finally discovers the old recluse and takes his counsel, he says in parting, "I've stubbed my toe and hurt my heel finding you. My army will pave a path in soft leather through the woods to make my way to you easier next time."

The wise man offers him a pair of soft leather moccasins.

"Try these instead."

The prince sees the folly of his ways and thanks the old man.

In the attitude of entitlement that the prince represents, nature is there to be bent to his will. However, he doesn't see the futility or tragedy of his position; like any demanding child, he merely wants the forest floor covered so he can walk around his kingdom barefoot, the sooner the better. In the attitude of stewardship that the wise man represents, it's much more agreeable to wear soft leather on one's feet and leave the woods alone.

In terms of attitude, the young prince seeks to change the outer world to fit his demanding specifications; the forest man, knowing this is a losing hand, suggests the prince change his inner world, his disposition about wearing shoes, for it is sure to provide better success.

Although obvious when put this way, we are so often like Prince Barefoot, making ludicrous demands on other people as well as ourselves. Heracles passed twelve impossible trials, but we can't pave a path through the forest any more than we can cleanse the Augean stables or capture the Cretan bull. We can't bend steel in our bare hands or change the course of mighty rivers.

All we *can* change is our attitude. That's it.

From our feelings about our weight, age, looks or career to our view of our partner, child, in-laws or community, the change in our attitude about the issue is what produces the desired outcome in us and for us. It starts by answering a question: who is responsible for you and what you do?

Crazy as it may sound, thinking you have no say makes it so.

This is the power of the words we tell ourselves. As long as he-she-or-they made you do it, you're a victim of an outcome over which you have no control. It's out of your hands. Those incompetent clowns have made a mess of your life again.

Blaming others feels good at first, but it won't stop your weight gain, bring back your missed career opportunity or patch up last night's argument. YOU are going to have to make that happen. Blaming no one is a better beginning, and by accepting responsibility for your behavior you take the first step toward a more pragmatic attitude. If YOU made you do what you did, then YOU can unmake and re-make what you do. After all, are you your behavior or are you the agency that can change your behavior?

When you acknowledge that a behavior is simply a learned response to a stimulus, that there are indeed many possible responses to a situation, you wake up to choices and put yourself in the driver's seat. In the same sense that you can select one of the many roads that lead to home, which behavior you choose is in no one's hands but your own.

Sure, all that hoopla about the sacrifices you have to make and the martyrdom you have to endure and the fools you must suffer now may look pretty silly to you, but it's looked silly to your loved ones and your work crew for a lot longer! I've logged plenty of time playing my own shame-blame-and-maim game, but two mentors, both named Barbara, helped inspire me to "chunk the junk" and re-tune myself toward an attitude of gratitude. They modeled behaviors of overwhelming generosity that showed me that in order to change my state of mind I had to change my base of thought.

Barbara Hailey, a talented director of children's theater and an amazing story teller who can move an audience with her sincere passion, wrote a couple of children's books about growing up with self-esteem that Chuck and I raised our children on. Barbara was also the second wife of a Dallas divorcee, Walter Hailey (see Attitude Step Nine), and I remember the stories she shared about his adult children and her role in their lives.

I was searching for encouragement on how to be a better "bonus mom" to Chuck's three daughters from a previous marriage, and I knew that Barbara's challenges with her husband's children exceeded mine. Mild mannered and gracious, she caught me off guard one afternoon when she told me, "If you love your husband, then you must love his children and you must come to respect and love their mother. It's worked for me."

"You've learned to love the woman whose scorn hell hath no fury for?"

"I admit it was a little tough for me at the beginning but by inviting all of Hailey's children as well as his ex-wife to Christmas dinner every year, we've all come to a brave, new understanding."

"I thought our family was open-minded with my siblings' loving embrace of one another from different parents but his ex-wife sitting at your table—that's really far out to me! You're a greater woman than I, Barbara."

"Not really. Opening my heart and home unconditionally is what helps me stay so happily married."

My attitude was defensive because my base of thought was fear driven. Here I was with kid gloves on trying not to slight or feel slighted in my role as an extra mom while this woman just threw all that propriety out the window and loved unconditionally. Her attitude was open and welcoming because her base of thought was to heal. It was an attitude, I came to learn, that she didn't just try on but applied to every situation she faced.

The generosity of spirit shining through her reminded me of another mentor I had met years earlier when I was just starting out in my career, Barbara Hopkins. A great cook, family matriarch and a real nurturer who reminds me of my mother, she worked diligently in the home keeping her oil executive husband and four grown sons on task. A few years into our friendship her husband died suddenly of a heart attack. He was only in his fifties, but she took care of everything in her competent, organized way.

I soon became a daughter figure to her and she became a mentor to me. I knew how to hunt and fish; she knew how to be a lady in life and in business. Her savvy helped me become nice and knowledgeable during a time in my life when I was sort of nice and all together totally naïve.

She had a natural elegance and was the epitome of class in everything she did. Her shoe closet was something this East Texas girl could only dream of, neatly assembled in color and order of heel height. A collector of fine jewelry, she saw me one day with my jaw dropped, staring at a South Sea China pearl ring with baguette diamonds that was especially breathtaking to me since I'm a June baby and this was my birthstone.

"You're going to the theatre in downtown Houston on Friday?"

"Why, Barbara?"

"Because you'll look great in that ring."

"I was thinking of going, but I can't wear that! No way!"

"Yes way, you can, Jo An."

"I'm aghast you caught me gaping at it like a school kid."

"Nonsense. I insist."

My attitude was defensive for my base of thought was shame. Her attitude was encouraging for her base of thought was to share. She'd been around this block a few times and knew that wearing something so stunning would have an effect upon a country girl like me and she was right. I truly felt beautiful, womanly and elegant that night. Of course I also worried my head off about the hardware, and it wasn't until I got into the theatre that I put to rest the fear that someone might take my finger off just to get this one-of-a-kind work of art.

A few years later we went into business together, and I saw on a daily basis that an attitude of generosity was the key to everything she did. We've stayed close over the many rivers we've crossed, but she's still capable of surprising me. On my fortieth birthday, a package arrived with a card that read, "You're very exceptional and today I want you to know how exceptional you are to me. Wear this and stand tall. Enjoy, your friend, Barbara."

Thinking it was so like Barbara to give me a perfect pair of heels, I had to sit down for fear of fainting because when I opened the package I found, tucked inside a red tissue-wrapped case, the South Sea China pearl ring with baguette diamonds along with its papers signed over to me.

I could hear her in my mind's ear saying, "I insist." I learned to change my mind regarding what others are capable of and what others will do.

*The ring from Barbara Hopkins extreme*
*EncourageMentor to JoAn*

## Attitude Step 8

# GIVING UP IS NOT AN OPTION

To an encourager, giving up is not an option but a mistake in perception. It's too focused on the pain, the "ow right now," to see the larger picture unfolding, that in the chrysalis of defeat and discouragement are born a butterfly's beautiful wings to a brighter future of gathering nectar from fragrant blossoms.

Not only a blunder and a blinder, giving up is also a fine how-do-you-do to what got you here. As we say in Texas, dance with the one that brung ya, and by that I mean celebrate the fortitude and stamina you discovered when overwhelming struggle first tried to stare you down and could not.

That's your strength, and the memories of your past failures are what motivate your future success. I'm talking about failures powerful enough to transform us, to rock our worlds, to grow us up fast because we won't survive repeating them again.

That's why a thorough knowledge of failure is success's best friend. The more failure we learn from, the more success we create. That's why giving up ruins everything. The reason the plot thickens and the game gets rough in our personal and professional lives is so that our virtue can arise in measure to the enormity of the task.

This moment of truth is about an inner resourcefulness, an ability to stand up to our own defeat. All my EncourageMentors over the years have held one thing in common: unlike me, caught up in the moment, everything on the line, fear and anxiety clouding my mind, they've never cared if I win or lose. They only care that I'm giving it all I've got, that the game inspires my ultimate performance. They know that for me to play my best is to beat defeat, independent of the final score.

However, my greatest EncourageMentors look to see if the issue causing me to want to quit has the power to make me re-think my own mission statement and life purpose. Invariably, when I see my own larger mission contrasted by the smallness of the moment in which I am entrapped, the attitude adjustment I need to make is simple and clear: instead of giving up, give the situation some patience. Whether a business or personal relationship, a family crisis or a career challenge, one of the risks of a passionate nature is a now-or-never sense of urgency, and I can vouch for the value of a wait-and-see approach with a little built-in breathing room. As Rainer Maria Rilke wrote, "Be patient toward all that is unsolved in your heart and try to love the questions themselves, like locked rooms and like books that are now written in a very foreign tongue. Do not now seek the answers, which cannot be given you because you would not be able to live them. And the point is, to live everything. Live the questions now."

This kind of patience is built on grit or resilience, and learning to hang tough and hang in there was bred into my core by my mother. In her last week of life she shared with me a story about a man throwing her out of a moving car in Houston while she was seven months pregnant. Had that been me, I would have given up on men. She, on the other hand, knew in her heart that there was a better future for her and she didn't give up until she found that better way with a more loving man. My father never stopped wanting to please her and remained affectionate with her throughout their long years together. I can't pretend to know why she never gave up on finding a better future, but never giving up on each other was the lesson they both taught me.

Now my brother-in-law Frank, the oil and gas worker in Attitude Step One, is learning this lesson hard and up close. In spite of back pain, he had not missed work and had been taking some injections to keep the discomfort at bay. However, with all the finger-pointing going on in the Gulf, his boss in Wyoming felt he shouldn't be a liability and forced him to have surgery by placing him on light duty, which would not cover expenses at his makeshift home in Wyoming and his permanent home in Texas. So he went home on short-term disability to have the surgery, but problems arose and the procedure was to be redone after a first attempt. When his requests for help were not answered by the on-call physician over the weekend following the second surgery, he showed up on Monday morning in disbelief to find that, thanks to whatever medical mishap had happened, he now was in a full-on fight against an MRSA infection, something we'd all heard horror stories about.

For four full weeks every day twice a day at 6:00 a.m. and 6:00 p.m., he went to the hospital for strong intravenous antibiotics often times adding a morphine drip for the pain he was experiencing. His situation had become a nightmare. Meanwhile the few returned calls from his boss indicated that the company was considering laying him off instead of extending his disability. His pain was now worse than when he started. The PICC line, now a mess, the medical team could no longer get blood samples from it and had to stick him in an arm every time they needed to draw blood.

As the treatments wound down to the last week, he returned to have his surgeon give him more bad news. The fluid had returned to the incision area and needed to be drained before a third operation was possible. A trip to a Houston neurosurgeon for a second opinion put it all in context. "You're in bad shape," he said, "and you need to go back to your first doctor and have him place two catheters to drain that fluid off your spine. It could still be dormant MRSA. When it is all gone, come back to me and we'll talk about extensive surgery with a fusion and pins but no guarantee as to the outcome." He returned to the original surgeon to hear he wouldn't do the requested procedure.

Knowing that issues can arise when one is laid off with no insurance and no time line for surgery or recuperation, Frank and Renee tried to refinance their home only to be told that the bank wouldn't budge because an internal flood in the house had damaged the ceiling and carpet. They admitted that they had real money concerns to even consider these repairs—indeed, that's why they sought financial help—but the bank would not consider a refinance until they made these repairs.

It was Catch 22 meeting the classic bait-and-switch. It looked as if the gas company, the bank, the insurance rep, the surgeon and the hospital were in a conspiracy to beat, cheat and bamboozle, but Frank and Renee chose to see it differently.

"My back trouble, loss of work, concerns about money and awareness of mortality has strengthened us as a couple and caused us to re-visit our values and our own vows to one another," Frank told me. "I couldn't do this without Renee. She's my strength and why I will never give up."

Funny, that's what my mom used to say about my dad. He ended by saying, "We can't give up. Somewhere there is somebody who is worse off than I am!"

*JoAn's sister and brother in-law*
*at a healthier time*

Attitude Step 9

# EXPOSE THE ELEPHANT
# IN THE ROOM

At one point in my career as a speaker, I had the opportunity to work alongside the late Walter Hailey, former MC of the Light Crust Doughboys, Texas Music Hall of Famer and legendary presenter. Irreverent and unpredictable, he was a wizard of wit, a lovable grandpa, a sagey old coot and a charismatic EncourageMentor to the huge audiences he commanded all over the United States and Canada.

In fact, the bigger the house, the better he played. On stage he was very joyously living his own press kit, a retiree who over the last fifty years had turned his personal adversities into plusses that tallied millions of dollars. Sitting in his seminar, you got the impression that no matter how far fetched your own dream might be, if Itsy Bitsy Hailey—short, insecure, afraid of rejection—could realize his, so could you. It was a unique transmission of confidence and a permission to fulfill your own sense of promise.

He had an uncanny sense of intuiting what his audiences were thinking and his greatest asset as a speaker was to expose the elephant in the room, to welcome into the conversation the uncomfortable subject that no one else wanted to address. By focusing on the thing his audience most preferred to avoid, his humorous banter lightened the mood. After he got through with the bad news no one wanted to talk about, it didn't look so bad.

It wasn't spin-doctoring; it was ju-jitsu. By getting the audience's subconscious content out in the open, he broke the ice, shared laughs and moved everyone past the danger. What might have become a distraction ended up being the bond that brought people together. His preference to disclose reminded me of one of my most useful principles, one that I believe is close to the heart of every EncourageMentor: "If you tell me something before I find it out from another source, it's information; if you tell me after, it's an excuse."

I coach, train and present regularly to manufacturers, laboratories, private practices and corporate teams in (and out of) dentistry. My husband Chuck is a dentist, and for many in my audience, that's a huge elephant, one that takes up all the room in the place. I know I'm not going anywhere with these folks, especially the young gals on dental teams, until I talk out what's on their minds. The range of suspicious thoughts can run from "What did she do in dentistry before she married him?" or "Does this dentist's wife really know anything about this industry?" to "Did she sleep her way to the front of the stage?" or "What gives her permission to speak?"

"I have university training but no degrees," I like to say up front to my audience, "and I started twenty-five plus years ago in the same trenches you are in now and learned and earned my way to the privilege of speaking to you; that in spite of the many positions I have held in the industry or certifications and auxiliary training titles I hold with well known institutes, the only real permission to speak that I have and the only reason I get invited back to speak is because of the difference I hope to make in your lives. So please don't confuse me with someone who doesn't care about you; you are why I am here. As for me and no degree, I've got nothing to hide behind so I better be effective."

Since the biggest fear for many in my audience is that, by being married to a dentist I can't begin to know how they feel working for one, I joke with them about being the dentist's wife. Instead of pretending everything's fine, this simple gesture of exposing the elephant in the room defuses trouble before it can get any momentum. Through poking fun I can take my audience's temperature and create a whole new level of conversation.

So much of the mess we make in our personal lives stems from not addressing the elephant in the room, which only grows bigger because of your silence. It's like going out on a date with a single man who has no children and not sharing with him that you have two wonderful kids. Whatever the outcome of the evening, by letting the facts be known, that you are a mother who will most likely be attached to her kids (and their father) for the length of your life, the sooner you can move forward. If the gentleman caller still thinks he is going to replace those kids or any part of the history that made them, he's not listening. It's not going to happen.

I often share with my audience the words my husband said to me at the beginning of our courtship, "This can be a great relationship as long as you understand you will never take the place of my three little girls and they deserve every moment I can give them." I know that many women would have been soooo turned off by his comment, but for me it edified my choice in this man. He was the epitome of a father, which is exactly what I would want if I had children—and which so pleased me when we did have a child. There was an added benefit, too. Many times early in our marriage we did not agree on a direction, but we did agree that we would always do what was right and best for the kids.

The point about approaching the unapproachable conversation is that you never know how it will play out except that it's better to speak than remain silent. In the last few years of her life, my mother was in a wheel chair. My son, five and a half when she passed away, cannot remember her without a wheel chair and a paralyzed left hand and leg, but even today he will speak to someone in a wheel chair and look directly into the individual's eyes, not necessarily at the body. He learned this valuable lesson from my mother as all of us did. She liked to say, "Me ah know ah my body a-messed up but ah please ah look a-my eyes."

It was her elephant in the room, and once she said it, it gave us the strength to expose our elephants in the room as well.

Attitude Step 10

# MANAGE YOUR OWN MORALE

Encouragement is a never-ending exchange of motivation, respect, awe, insight, engagement, admiration, support, prompt, care, inspiration, enthusiasm, discernment, kindness, esteem, delight, comprehension, thoughtfulness, incentive, stimulation, solidarity, empathy, enjoyment, consideration, impetus, appreciation, challenge, compassion, alliance, understanding, selflessness, wonder, value, harmony, tolerance, perception, collaboration and camaraderie between the mentor and the mentored.

Morale is the fuel that keeps the fire of encouragement ablaze. The great mentors know how precious and scarce morale can be, especially in taxing times. So they naturally gravitate toward meta-mentors who manifest a confident can-do-ness. Those who can manage their own morale are the true masters of encouragement. Not only have they learned and grown through the give-and-take exchanges they encounter in mentoring, they've found an inner light or source that keeps their outer lamp trim and bright, a beacon for the discouraged.

When my own morale is flagging, I find solitude to be the best medicine for what's bugging me. It's Phase One of my approach. I like to wake up early before other duties command my attention and go to an undisturbed part of the house in order to spend a little time alone and with (almost) no interruption from bells, whistles, phones, faxes, tweets, timers and computers. Surrounded by inspiring books and beautiful art that I love as well as plenty of peace and quiet, I look introspectively for insight on the person, place or thing that is challenging me. I read and highlight passages, I jot notes and write responses, I contemplate and reflect, pray and meditate. Before I comment or give an opinion, I ask myself: what is my role in what has just happened and what is the desired outcome?

When I have a grasp of this, I start on Phase Two of my approach, talking it through with a few close friends (and a terrific life partner) who have no fear about giving me the skinny on how I could do things differently to have a better result. Their feedback is invaluable, and since I trust where they are coming from and know that they love me, I've learned not to fight the information or get ugly behind it but let it sink in slowly.

As soon as it does, I begin Phase Three, returning to the event that tested my morale and delivering hope to others in whatever form appropriate. I make an offer, an opening, a beginning of an exchange of ideas—not a one-time-only, take-it-or-leave-it monologue. When the discussion gets interesting and both of us are more intrigued with possibilities than when we started, I move into Phase Four—giving my listener sincere compliments—before ending the conversation.

This approach works well for me because it allows me to fix the flaw in my own morale. I know my morale is on me and not the stuff I make up about other people, so instead of jumping in with my guns blazing when I'm upset, the four phases causes me to slow down and consider many sides of the puzzle, not just my own.

That's still only half the story. Besides an understanding family and a system of feedback loops to check and balance my enthusiasms, I have a fantastic team that works with me, not for me. They are all managers of their own morale who abide by Gandhi's insight, "The best way to find yourself is to lose yourself in the service of others." Service distinguishes all that they do, and in service there is no ego.

Instead of knowing what I know and staying away from what I don't know, I've learned to get a taste of the tasks I'm not good at for they have revealed to me the talents I lack and the jobs that I need to delegate. In addition to humbling me, this method reminds me of how valuable all the tasks are, from answering the phone to prospecting creatively for clients, and when I find the person who excels with love and talent at the tasks I hate or just can't do well, I'm thrilled.

I may shine from the stage but it's no understatement that for me the devil is in the details, and speaking-coaching-training engagements, mailings, brochures, hotel accommodations, shipping deadlines, word counts, spell checks, fee collections, on-site requirements, internet presence, flight schedules and follow-ups are chockfull of details. When I arrive at a seminar venue and there is nothing for me to worry about—every single thing has been taken care of, the handouts and reading materials are there ahead of me all in order and everyone who signed up is present and accounted for—that is the beauty of working with folks who are smarter and more organized than me.

Jeannie is not only my assistant, event coordinator, web gal, detail detective and trouble-shooter with a background in accounting, she foresees where dilemmas might arise, re-routes us and takes a safer course. In the past I'd worked for companies for whom the client's success and well being were not Job One and when I went into business for myself I insisted this was the only way to go. Jeannie really helped make that happen. She's as capable as I am to make many of the day-to-day decisions, and I can hand her the company checkbook without fear.

Because her focus is on our clients' concerns, not a preconceived sense of power or status, she's more interested in the VFP (valuable final product) than being the one with the right or wrong answer. This creates a synergy that is unmistakably magnificent. When she brings in Sandi, a graphics genius who makes my ideas look magical on paper, and the rest of our team for a brainstorming session, it feels as if our brain waves and heart waves, our concepts and implementations and our connections and inspirations grow exponentially.

If that was all my team could do for me, I would be in hog heaven, but it doesn't end there. Everyone on the team is living in their own personal lives the message that our company promotes. This makes my going to work feel more like I'm in a mastermind alliance than at a job.

No one is afraid to bring up what's really happening, and everyone on the team gladly helps cover my weaknesses so that I can soar with my strengths. For example, Jeannie can put my Achilles' heel—I'm not just geographically dumbfounded, I'm directionally challenged!—in a favorable light. When I'm traveling I love a GPS, but what I love more than a GPS is a driver! Jeannie will often share with a client, "You'll love what she can do from the front of the room, but if you want her to arrive to do it, you should get a car service, not a rental car!" Instead of apologizing for my limitation, she's able to enroll the client in helping me get where I need to go.

One of the most outstanding benefits of our team walking its talk is that people call our office many, many times needing help with a difficult discussion. That's how I got nicknamed "the conversation coach." I advise clients to stick to systems that keep the blame off people for this makes it easier to look at thorny situations. With the focus on the outcome, people are more willing to open up and consider other points of view. This is the heart of all great coaches and servant leaders: understanding the desired outcome and inspiring everyone to work toward it.

Although I'm fortunate to have a great team, do not think that you need to wait for the right person or cadre of enthusiastic workers before you can realize success. By managing your own morale you raise the bar yourself and begin to attract people just like you, folks ready, willing and able to grow your product or service's greatest opportunity.

# Attitude Step 11

# ENDLESSLY QUEST FOR LEARNING

W hen our son was seven years old, he came in one day late in the afternoon from playing with some friends in the yard. My husband was watching a training video of a dental implant procedure when our son inquired, "Dad, do we have to watch teeth tonight?"

I was laughing so hard I could hardly cook. This is what our son has seen since he was old enough to remember: his dad watching educational videos on his day off, reading at night in bed, joining study clubs and going to seminars and retreats to improve his value to his industry and to our family.

Chuck is one of the most dedicated lifetime learners I know. He doesn't just treat his professional life this way; he reads equally as much material on being a better father to a son and a better husband to a career wife. He even listens to books on CD when he drives long distances.

He's great to be around because life is a learning adventure with him. He practices a CANI mindset, that is, Constant And Never-ending Improvement. One of its main principles is to raise one's own standards. As Tony Robbins writes, "If you're waiting for someone else to raise your standards, you should write your epitaph now because it's probably not going to happen."

Chuck knows that by creating value in yourself, you become more valuable to others. I first saw this illustrated at a conference we attended that I will never forget. We hadn't been married long and we were still getting to know each other's ways. On this particular occasion, the presenter had lost me early on. It wasn't just the bowtie or the monotone drone of his delivery or the list of his famous accomplishments; it was his disregard for his audience. He lectured as if we weren't there—he never even paused or expressed interest in any feedback. At one point he accidentally queried, "Are there any questions before I move on?"

Chuck raised his hand and respectfully asked for some clarity about a particular slide the guy had covered in detail versus a particular article the guy had written in a journal that contradicted this.

"I'll cover that individually at the break," he droned, "I need to move on now." At the break the guy made a bee line to Chuck.

"Do you really read all those articles and remember that stuff?"

"Yes, sir, I do."

"Look, I didn't actually write the article that you read, and you are right. It does contradict what I teach but I was asked to put my name on it and I guess I forgot what it said."

The guy was flushed with embarrassment. Chuck had peeped his hole card!

As the day ended we went down to the bar to have a drink before dinner. This group of guys and gals had been in the same classes for several months so they knew each other pretty well, and I could tell they had discussed the professors they were hearing every weekend in class together. This was the first time I had driven up to hear any of it due to my travel schedule, but we wanted to have a nice day and a dinner together and this seemed like an opportunity. As soon as we sat down, several of the folks in class found their way to our little table to ask Chuck questions. The material taught needed a little discussion to be fully digested and Chuck had provided what the guy had not—an opportunity to bounce the ideas around until they made better sense. In doing so, he became a person of value to his class, and at that moment I knew I wanted to be a lifetime learner as well.

I wasn't a particularly great student in school, nor was I a fast reader. I have always been curious although I never cared much for books about a "make believe" life. I've preferred books that keep it real and make it attainable. Since I dream about the possibilities of doing life better, reading has always given me an opportunity to review, renew and improve upon my life and my family and business relationships.

However, listening to my husband talk to our children turned a light on for me. He said that until they learned to read for their own enjoyment, instead of doing it for an assignment, they were missing out on the better part of the experience. I then realized that all of my reading time had been practical and assignment-driven in nature. Now I saw new possibilties in reading for pleasure.

I could do it just for me.

I could reap the rewards and find joy in the pages for just that reason, finding joy, getting caught up in the story and ending up feeling renewed and wiser at the end. It was another kind of learning, not merely a diversion or an entertainment but a human narrative that opened the heart and the imagination. My curiosity had found a new outlet. I soon was reading more widely in my down-time (fun and entertainment) as well as in my up-time (education and improvement) and also began to share more books with others, folks I was seeking to encourage or draw encouragement from.

Reading a book is such a personal, solitary experience, but sharing that experience with others can provide great insight. Some of the best encouragement has come not from the book, but from what the book triggered in discussion with friends, colleagues and mentors afterward.

Below is a short list of some of my favorite titles, classic chestnuts and the latest word, that have been known to trigger a few powerful ideas and cause a stir in my circle:

*Acres of Diamonds* by Russell Conwell

*As A Man Thinketh* by James Allen

*A Whole New Mind: Why Right Brainers Will Rule The World* by Daniel Pink

*Glimpses of Heaven* by Trudy Harris

*Life@Work* by John Maxwell

*Our Iceberg Is Melting: Changing and Succeeding Under Any Conditions* by John Kotter

*Purple Cow* by Seth Godin

*Sticks & Stones Exposed: The Power of Your Words* by Dave Weber

*The Five Love Languages* by Gary Chapman

*The Heart of a Leader & The One Minute Apology* by Ken Blanchard

*The Leader Who Had No Title* by Robin Sharma

*The Power of Nice & The Power of Small* by Kaplan Thayler

*Think and Grow Rich* by Napoleon Hill

One of the greatest habits worth cultivating is the gift of endless learning. It's not just about reading books or attending continuing education courses but about a point of view that responds to other people's success and good fortune by asking how their remarkable idea can become one's own idea—and how to avoid their failures and pitfalls as well. It's a matter of linking and synching what has worked valuably for others and making an application that advances your own intent with your career, family and community.

I would propose to you, no matter what your life or business circumstances, everything you need to be successful already exists; you just haven't been exposed to it. That exposure is found in books and in people.

As the late Charlie "Tremendous" Jones used to say, "You're the same today as you'll be in five years except for two things: the books you read and the people you meet."

# Attitude Step 12

# NO ONE TAKES A BACK SEAT

T*he Leader Who Had No Title* by Robin Sharma is one of my favorite reads, one I go back to again and again, because it encourages you to be a leader in what you do, no matter what your station in life may be. You don't have to be the owner to think like the owner and you don't have to be the top dog on the team to enrich the team or influence a more favorable outcome.

You just have to lead by your own example.

If you're waiting for your boss, manager or business owner to give you props and accolades, consider these words your ultimate permission statement: find the accolade in the job itself by doing it with your professional best.

It's like the lesson in Attitude Step Three, instead of waiting for someone else to care, initiate care yourself. No one takes a back seat to helping create a team environment. To make your team more conducive to problem solving, build trust and respect by listening with an open mind and forgiving heart what people say to you.

I'm reminded of a story that Karen, assistant principal at a large Texas high school, told me of John, a high school student who not only took a back seat to learning—he got lost in the process.

"A nice looking, polite young man with an incredible smile and bright, happy eyes," Karen told me, "John frequently hung out with a group of gang wannabes, even though he didn't quite fit. Eventually, he started showing up in my office for typical freshman disciplinary situations like tardiness and cutting classes to more serious offenses later.

"As I got to know him, the more puzzled I became as to what was actually the motive behind his constant acting out. For reasons unknown to me at the time, John seemed relieved to be sent to my office away from his peers. When I asked why he was always getting in trouble, he merely shrugged his shoulders and said, 'I don't know why I do those things; I just do.' His teachers couldn't figure him out either.

"The breakthrough came after he'd been sent to my office for classroom misbehavior. I shook my head, asked him the same payoff question I'd asked so many times before, issued him his consequences and sent him back to class. Shortly after he left, I heard a faint knock. I opened the door, and there was he standing with an anxious look on his face. 'Can I talk to you?' he whispered. 'I need to tell you something that I've never told anyone before.' 'Come on in and sit down,' I told him.

"I wondered what John had to say, for fear he might tell me he had done something illegal. 'Do you know why I get in trouble? If I'm in a computer class, for example, and I've got students on either side of me working on an assignment, I talk with one of them because I can't read. I can't even start the assignment as I have no idea of what to do, so instead, if I get in trouble, I can leave the classroom and not feel embarrassed about not being able to read.'

"I knew John was regarded as being dyslexic but had absolutely no idea that he couldn't read. 'Let me look into this,' I told him. After sharing his story with the principal, I researched John's previous testing and discovered that not one teacher had tested him for a reading disability. As a result, my school's specialists tested John and discovered he not only had a learning disability, but that he also had hearing loss in one ear.

"With a lot of encouragement and support from numerous educators, John successfully graduated from high school and secured permanent employment. I recently ran into him at his job and he expressed thanks for the chance to turn his life around since that fateful day in my office."

Karen's willingness to solve a problem the rest of John's educators had failed to find only underlines the best of what it means to lead with a service-driven purpose. The capacity is within all of us, and has everything to do with being effective and nothing to do with job title or alleged status. Plus, Karen exemplified the best of what I call servant leadership: she got her knees dirty.

Servant leadership is a less restrictive model, one that shakes up roles and allows teams and families to enjoy duties or deeds that can be spread out. No one really is afraid of what they might be asked to do because most servant leaders are happy to have done it or at least to try it. That's what I love about the TV show, Undercover Boss. They take CEOs and put them into their own businesses at an entry level position in order to get the skinny on what others in the company think about how management works. When they find out that the guy who's been working right beside them for a couple of weeks is really the CEO undercover, they are blown away. Tears of joy are shed when the CEOs openly recognized team member's achievements, dedication and loyalty, often rewarding unsuspecting team members with promotions based on what they learn while serving the company they run.

One episode offered the information to the CEO that this particular young woman couldn't afford her needed medical care on the wages she made. It was a real eye opener. Another allowed the CEO to see the sexual harassment one of his appointed general managers was serving up at one location.

This is a whole other conversation than the usual one we're so often caught up in, the one about making others feel less than by bragging on oneself, one's stuff or one's children. When you feel or see that a change is needed or desired for a different outcome, try the permission statement rather than the boasting statement.

"Do I have permission to be honest with you about something?" Or, "Do I have permission to coach you?" Asking the team, spouse or child for permission creates a pause in the action that can have the person listening differently as you offer information differently. It opens the line of communication and makes it clear that, no matter one's role or part, no one really takes a back seat in the conversation—or in life.

Wintley Phipps is a world-renowned education activist, Grammy nominated musician, motivational speaker, pastor, and founder of the U.S. Dream Academy, a national after-school and mentoring program that has helped thousands of at-risk youth realize their dreams, but it's not his accomplishments that I want to share.

It is a simple remark he made at the closing of one of his engagements to a young girl who reached out to him and shared with him her feeling less than adequate. After prayer, he told her that the Lord had laid on his heart to share that she was to be an important and influential person. She turned out to be the greatest EncourageMentor of our time. Her name is Oprah Winfrey, and that one act from that one person now stretches and reaches and encourages millions near and far. You never know who you're talking to until you discover who they become.

As Albert Camus said, "Real generosity toward the future lies in giving all to the present."

Attitude Step 13

# TAKE THE HIGH ROAD

Taking the high road has always felt downright uncomfortable. When I've been wronged or hurt by someone or something, it feels more natural to heal the wound by righting the wrong. When pushed, I want to push back.

I grew up reading the New Testament, and I've always been challenged by the phrase Jesus spoke at the Sermon on the Mount, "Turn the other cheek," the notion of responding to an aggressor without violence. Socrates expressed an analogous sentiment in his dialogue with Crito before his execution in Athens, "One should never do wrong in return, nor mistreat any man, no matter how one has been mistreated by him." This moral principle guided Socrates to the conclusion that he should not attempt to escape from punishment despite being wrongfully imprisoned.

Guided by a moral principle! I know the concept isn't new but it's certainly due for a comeback. In fact philosophers the world over, both ancient and modern, have come to the same conclusion: let go of the hostility and transcend the conflict.

I knew I was missing something because I kept thinking about this in terms of winners and losers and turning the other cheek seemed like a loser's hand—until I heard Joyce Landorf speak. She said there are two kinds of people with two kinds of vision: those in the balcony and those in the basement. Balcony people tend to keep their head up and their eyes are on the long term and the fuller story. They're more likely to take the high road during adversity because they see the bigger picture with a better perspective as well as with greater nuance. Basement people are less inclined to look up, to check a forecast or to think about consequences. They don't have time to plan their evacuation. Adversity has already found them waddling in the depths and bumping about in the dark without much of a clue.

Now I understood. The insight of Socrates, Jesus, Buddha, Confucius and the other wise and wide-angled seers the world over was that taking the high road was a better and more informed choice, not a loser's losing bet. It was the adult thing to do. I saw from their vantage point that taking the high road was really taking the shorter route, the one that acknowledged that a response of vengeance, violence or evening the score was just more of the ignorance that had turned us against one another in the first place. Moreover, the high road was all that these philosophers had in order to model a sane and kind behavior to the rest of us. It was an act of tolerance in the face of abuse, not a collapse into weakness, and an inspiration to all who had been wronged for it led one out of the prison of retribution and self-righteousness and into new possibilities.

It made great sense to me for the first time, but it wasn't until I felt mortally and morally wronged that I understood how liberating taking the high road can be. Well, I didn't go through it all that gently; kicking and screaming was more like it, but I did make it to the other side of the equation: I didn't want to strike back. It just took me awhile. I had to let the volcano cool.

My industry is relatively small, and most of the people teaching, training, certifying and coaching doctors and teams know one another. We meet at the same conferences, study groups and institutes and we read the same periodicals. I started to run the idea by a few of the best and brightest that we could have more impact as a team than we could separately.

What we held in common as presenters was a team model and each of us was an all-star at her position. Although I may have been the biggest rainmaker, that is, I could enroll larger numbers of folks in presentations, the idea was that we could all help make rain for one another, that together we could bring in more business and have a greater impact for good in our industry. This was my first mistake. Little did I know that some of my team members weren't interested in building a company. Some thought of me, the team leader, as their booking agent and personal rainmaker.

Well, right out of the box we had a catastrophe. We no sooner donned our signature red jackets for our first seminar then we realized a company we'd done business with was now bankrupt. With checking accounts weak, some panicked. I ought to have paid more attention to this growing fissure in the group—a few felt used and abused and some felt we'll just do better next time—but I was trying to make rain, working night and day to line up gigs for us all.

A more mature leader would have wondered why no one else on the team was on the phone running down speaking engagements, getting the word out about our new remarkable organization and securing our future, but I felt so responsible for the lost fees that I ended up bailing out the company, thanks to a loan from my husband.

The next year looked more hopeful, but just as we were delivering the seminar that could have gotten us well, I realized that our team was falling apart, not coming together! I walked into a meeting and was told by an unhappy teammate that I was not appreciative of her and the others and that if the money from the next year's program was not split with her that I was through.

How could I be flipped so quickly after negotiating a fairer salary for her a few years before? How could I be working daily with two of my team in and out my home office to fill the seats, take the many calls, run the cards, prepare the handouts, make the plans and presentations and all of a sudden someone who showed up that weekend on location counting seats was now demanding half the profits? Where was she when I was looking for money to bail us out the year before? I was extremely hurt.

My thoughts were: How can she fire me? I own the company, and I too have a relationship here. And how can she bring it up now? Then I shared with her, "These folks are expecting a great seminar and I am not going to address this again until we deliver what they came for. This meeting is over and I will take it all under advisement."

The seminar did go as well as I hoped, but it took some time for me to gather my thoughts after I returned home. I called on Joy Millis, a trusted advisor and extreme EncourageMentor to me in my life both business and personal. I told her how wounded I felt, how a company that had been built with so much blood, sweat and tears could be topped so easily by one malicious act. I ended the rant by saying, "What doesn't kill me is gonna make me stronger."

"Honey, what doesn't kill you, qualifies you. Keep serving."

It was the best encouragement I could have found. It helped me see that our company may be finished, but my service to this industry was not. My attorney drafted letters to all saying that the party was over and the thrill was gone. I wrote a check to everyone for their red jackets and dismantled the group.

It stung pretty badly at first but within several months I was on a call with a doctor who really needed training in an area that happened to be this particular ex-team member's proficiency. Sure, I could have delivered the training myself, but this was her expertise and she was the best in the business. So I gave the doctor her number.

As a courtesy, I called to give her the heads-up on the doctor I had recommended her to so that she would be prepared when he got in touch with her. She said she was surprised at my call and thanked me for the referral. She acknowledged the damage and lamented the teams that would never hear what we had to say and that no one was served by what had happened. She didn't think I would forgive her, much less send her work.

I suggested that I was not the one who was the judge, just someone who had found out that forgiveness has its own rewards. I added that I couldn't think of anyone as good as her and I wasn't going to let my issues in the past get in the way of this guy's needs in the present.

I decided to take the high road at that very moment and it was the only road that wasn't rocky.

We shared a laugh and I wished her the best. The heavens didn't open, nor was I swept up in an overwhelming sense of glory, but I had learned the meaning of turning the other cheek, and I found that I was grateful to her.

# OPEN THE DOOR

The biggest barrier to learning something new is so often our old learning. I've had a few close encounters with "mistaken certainties"—my own as well as other people's—that have taken a toll on my heart muscles and stomach lining, especially early in my career.

Having been raised by a father who thought my mother was "it" and wouldn't cross her for anything, he didn't just think his little girl hung the moon, he would have bet his life on it. Such an upbringing didn't prepare me for some gentlemen in our industry whose mistaken certainty told them that glass ceilings for women were just what the doctor ordered. Nor did it prepare me for working in and around prima donnas whose mistaken certainty told them that no one other than a doctor could possibly know or teach them anything. Indeed, I took a few bumps from butting my head up against the darned door before I actually opened it.

I represent teams and the power of teamwork in an industry that is still very hierarchal. Usually the dentist (employer) is male and the rest of the dental team is female (employee), and I help both parties get past viewing the other as oppositional and discover their roles as complementary. Although this model produces healthier patients, better bottom lines and a lively *esprit de corps*, some folks can't get to the good news.

Opening the door has allowed me to continue the search for the people who are searching for the good news. For example, several years ago I met a couple of young dentists at an institute where I train teams. Moved by my presentation, they thought that what I had to say about teams was mandatory for their team to hear and they asked me when could I come and speak with them. These guys were avid learners and wanted a team of learners working alongside them. They felt it was important to the results they would produce both in their practices and for their patients' outcomes that the team be aligned with their quest for learning.

What I was offered was a dream come true, an opportunity to create the kind of training I was talking about and that our industry was in dire need of, a team approach that grew the practice and the quality of life for the patient, doctor and team. Hey, what about my old learning of glass ceilings, Big Bubba Texas, doctors with cancer of the ego and an unspoken entitlement expectation that blinded good people from finding better ideas?

Justin Moody, my partner and friend in a new endeavor, is of a new generation that understands the power of a harmonious and vibrant team. He has an amazing vision that invites the value that others can bring to it. Light years ahead of his peers, his team concept is the reason he is attracting some of the greatest minds in dentistry today.

To find him, I had to open a door. Had I believed my own mistaken certainties, I would not have made it to the meeting that changed my life. Call me lucky, but spell luck Laboring Under Correct Knowledge. It just takes awhile to accumulate that knowledge. Chris Holden, president of Heraeus North America, is one of the smartest guys I know, someone with a quest for learning and one of the least likely to get jammed up by his own mistaken certainties, especially on the job, but it happened to him years ago. It was the first time Chris had ever worked for someone who was younger than he. His new boss—very bright, highly educated, suave and handsome—seemed to epitomize the phrase, "Life ain't fair." Chris couldn't quite get over how the guy always knew the right thing to say.

More so, this younger man could communicate without intimidation to anyone regardless of age or station in life. This was a bit of a challenge on the one hand but on the other, he was very bright.

These were life skills that Chris was in pursuit of, but he had to get past the hang-up that this person seemed to have everything going for him and had achieved more though he had less years of experience. He questioned his own mistaken certainty that he could not learn from someone younger than he, and realized that in order to learn, he had to get past his old habits of learning.

He told me that over the course of two and half years, the manager shared a number of valuable lessons, but three points were most important and remain with him to this day:

- What a person does for a living is not who they are, so treat everyone with the same level of respect and accommodation.

- Business would be really easy were it not for people; ironically, what business can exist without people? Therefore, see point 1.

- Never isolate yourself in your office. Get out and see people, be they customers or colleagues. All too often, leaders make the mistake of isolating themselves in their offices where they feel safe.

Once Chris started learning from the guy, he stopped thinking of him as younger. He conceded that age had never mattered; it had just been his habit to learn from older people. By learning from the younger and brighter man, his discomfort turned into admiration and his fear of being shown up by a boss younger than he turned into respect.

In short, he opened a door. He's been getting LUCKier ever since.

Attitude Step 15

# REVIEW CANDIDATES CONSTANTLY

Jack Dempsey, considered by some to be the greatest rough and tumble fighter who ever lived, held the world heavyweight title from 1919 to 1936. In addition to packing quite a knockout punch, he was known for bobbing and weaving, a style that made him a difficult target to hit solidly, both in and out of the ring. When asked, "What did you do to get so strong?," the Manassa Mauler gently replied, "Do you really want to know or are you asking just to ask?"

Like many of us, he faced a lot of questions in his day, but unlike most of us, he learned how to bob and weave around the query. It's not that he avoided giving an answer; he was finding out more about his interviewer's level of interest in order to give a more appropriate response.

We're trained by our parents and teachers to answer questions, but sometimes the best answer to a question is a question, isn't it? Many times we need to know more about what's hidden—an inference, implication or context—inside the question.

In Attitude Step Six, I shared my own discovery of the value of asking questions, and if you've been reading the book from Page One, you may have gathered that I'm not the right encourager for the helpless, lazy, nay-saying, fear-driven, complaint-crazy, energy-sucking team or family member who is a total drain at work or family reunions. I'm not saying that such persons aren't worth the invitation, only that I no longer feel that I must, will, want, should or can change them.

However, when they decide to change, I'm there and I'll take their call. In the meantime I choose to avoid the whining and pining and the huffing and puffing from the long-suffering and the embittered. They're not wrong, only people with whom I'm not likely to create a deep bond. I want to MSH, make stuff happen, not VSE, validate someone's excuse for failure.

I know that for me it is important when accepting requests to mentor that I review the candidate the same way Jack Dempsey handled questions. Actually, with or without a request, I review candidates constantly. I look for a person's ability to listen with a new set of ears, not the tired and defeated "I tried it that way" or the defensive "That won't work where I live or with my family" attitude. Searching out how open and attentive a candidate can be is necessary and courteous. Time is a valuable but limited resource and the only one we'll never get back, so we can all agree to use it wisely. In short, I look for a mentoree who has the drive and ambition to use the information I offer.

I met such a person a few years back, but I almost missed him at the time because he didn't quite fit what I thought I was looking for in a candidate. I love ice hockey, in spite of living in Texas, and I love giving workshops for coaches and players. It was at one such clinic in College Station that I met Nathan Banks, undergraduate, member of Texas A & M's ice hockey club and coach of my son's team one summer. Quiet and reserved, he introduced himself to me and I wondered why this young man would hardly make eye contact. My first thought was: what's a shrinking violet doing playing hockey on a team filled with daring young men whose families should glow in the dark because they have so much to be proud of?

These young ice hockey players did what they were supposed to do when they were supposed to do it with no debate. When they told the rink or youth hockey club that they would be there, they were there, on task and ready to "Git R' Done" as they say in Texas. These guys were just a really fine group of young men, the kind you would want your son to grow up and be like.

I stayed in touch with the team, and the following year Nathan was elected president of the Hockey Club. He called me up to share the news and asked me for several ideas and tips on communicating with the community, hockey parents, families, teammates and businesses to try to grow interest for the sport in Texas.

I began to mentor him in outreach ideas to produce better results for the club. Gone was the sheepish demeanor, the downcast eyes and the tight-lipped silence. Perhaps he only needed a little recognition before his leadership skills could emerge. Still, I wasn't sure what to expect. I shared suggestions but I didn't want to over-direct him or map out a step-by-step approach.

I soon found out there was no need. Nathan connected the dots by himself and found real success in using the systems for referrals and generating revenue that I outlined. He went from none to a great many favorable responses and donation pledges that year far exceeded any previous. Many times he has called to express both thanks and surprise when something I suggested about producing a particular response in someone worked. I often remind him, "Success is in the system, as W. Edwards Deming, the guy who invented the system, said."

While still in office, he even brought along the next year's president and his team of marketing guys to welcome them into the fold. He really took on the role like a real leader would, and since last year things have gotten even more interesting. Sean Boyle, who grew up in Alaska, is their new coach, and for the first time in Texas ice hockey history, a Texas team made it to the regional playoffs in Colorado Springs last year. Now the bar has been raised in many ways for the team this year.

Coach Boyle, like Nathan, is another open-minded learner with a quest to be his best. He has turned the community's attention to a sport that was virtually unknown through his influence he has on his players. An avid reader, he is constantly sharing insights and wisdom in areas of family, focus and sports. To me he is more than a coach because when he won a coaching award this past year he immediately turned the focus to his players who he said really won it.

Throughout the mentorship with Nathan, that's what I saw happening within him. He went from shy and self-conscious to lion-hearted and team-conscious. I didn't spoon-feed him, I only responded to his questions; I didn't suggest he raise his standard, he raised it all by himself through the results he produced.

That's what guided me when I looked for a mentor in my industry, someone both successful and significant in the area in which I wished to excel. I looked for results that resembled my own aspirations. Naomi Rhode has served and been honored in so many ways: she is in the CPAE Speaker Hall of Fame, a past president of both the National Speakers Association and the International Federation for Professional Speakers, a 1997 Cavett Award Winner and a recipient of the 2003 Legend of the Speaking Profession.

I was nervous when I asked her, but she agreed so wholeheartedly that I got over it in time to tell her that the ultimate respect for being mentored by the best is that I not monopolize her time. She assured me this would not happen and suggested we start with the first question I had for her.

It's a great way to find a mentor: ask. Ask questions, ask for advice, ask for help and ask for the experience of someone who has been where you are hoping to go.

Show initiative, be quick to give credit to those who helped you get this far and don't be afraid of no. That two-letter word only means keep looking. We're all at different points in our lives, families, and businesses and sometimes we have more time than other times. Just keep your eyes open and find the right ones for your long-term goals.

My longest and most fruitful business mentorship has been with Bob Vargo, a blessed man and living inspiration to me. A champion regional manager for Astra Tech, he has caused me to change my thinking about myself and my place in our industry. Thanks to his encouragement that began many, many years ago, I made it to the front of the room where my talents could be best put to service and use. He never fails to show up at my seminars, cheer me on and cause me to live my material.

I remember the day he walked into a dental practice that I was working for and suggested I ought to go to work for him. I shuttered at the thought and didn't know how in the world I could do that. He suggested I didn't know my own strengths yet. He taught me to take a risk and dared me to be all I could be. Over the years, when I was discouraged and felt myself to be at the mercy of other people's mistaken certainties, Bob would re-visit the first time he met me and remind me of how far we had come.

Janice Sloan, a team member in a seminar company many years ago and a valued friend still today, was the other industry insider who caused me to dream in Technicolor and then act on those (impossible) dreams. Detail oriented and very knowledgeable, she balances my skills and has been a great companion for me on stage and off. When I first tried to go it on my own as a speaker, trainer or coach, I couldn't really understand why someone would want to pay a fee to hear just little old me. So I sold the deal for the two of us often.

Janice knew I was afraid. She suggested I try it on my own and said, "I will do the seminar with you, but you need to learn that you don't need me or anyone else." It was the beginning of one of the greatest growth spurts

I've had in my speaking career. I trusted her emphatically and she trusted me which meant it was worth trying.

Finally, in seeking mentors of encouragement don't forget what Dr. Suess said: "Those who mind don't matter and those who matter don't mind."

## Attitude Step 16

# STAY CONNECTED

"Stay connected."

That was our mother's last request to us as she lay dying, that her family would always make time to be together. Nothing was more important to her than the bond our blended family had forged over the years.

So on the first anniversary of her death, we decided to hold a family reunion. My oldest sister Judy, who contends that after caring for all of us she has earned the right to say just about anything, sat us down to share stories of "back in the day." She never tires of pointing out some distinctive element of our mother in each of us. My next oldest sister Lou got our mother's ingenuity and tenacity to survive, my brother Al her most forgiving spirit and ability to find the good in others, my sister Renee her exquisite skill in the kitchen and garden with a spirit of service. By the way, Judy, like my mom, is one of the most beautiful women you'll ever meet—and has our mom's sense of style.

I always love hearing her tales because as the youngest and the only one born after my mom's stroke, there are things I never remembered her saying or doing. In fact Judy recently visited my webpage with the new video footage on it and called me up weeping.

"Jo, it's like I'm looking at our mother from years before. Your voice, your mannerisms, your sense of humor, your facial gestures, your inflection, the way you move all around the stage: you're just so much like her, it's scary. You command the room's attention just like she did. And what you teach about rapport—that's mother to a tee."

I was thrilled to hear this and started weeping, too. I can't remember my mother without broken speech and a limp or a wheelchair, so this was particularly gratifying, to know I am carrying some part of her indomitable spirit forward and sharing it with others.

I never felt prouder, nor more aware of my mother's wisdom. By asking us to stay connected, she knew that we would continue to draw upon each other's many strengths, the gifts we had gotten from her and our dad plus the years we've spent making our own lives and careers and nourishing our children with these same attitude steps. That's the encouragement she gave us, something that is replenished by giving, something to be shared and passed on down the generations.

Imagine that the words you are reading hold a secret charm and that by getting to the end of the sentence you could instantly come face-to-face with your greatest mentor of encouragement—who would that be?

Write that person a letter of thanks and acknowledgement. It is a noble and generous act to tell mentors of encouragement while they are alive how cherished they are to you, how what they said or did changed your life or your outlook for the better.

Take the time to write down the thing that you will wish you would have said on the anniversary of their death and do it now. Let them know how they have impacted you, how proud you are to stand on the shoulders of the stand they took, how their courage lives on in your outlook and in your actions and in the actions of those yet to be born.

You can never know how much it will mean until you know how much it meant. When my siblings and I went to prepare for my sweet daddy's funeral, it blessed my soul to find in his nightstand a tattered and torn letter that I had written him some ten years before and that he requested I read aloud at his funeral. I'd written him to thank him for everything he'd given me, of what a strong and supportive father he'd been to me, how his own living the lesson about hard work and preseverance had paid big dividends for me and how his love of the outdoors had stayed with me over the years. It was one of his proudest moments, to know how much his daughter admired him, and as he grew weak and his health grew complicated, he told me that he read the letter often to renew his strength. So take the time to "write the letter."

Connection is what the human spirit is all about.

Once you write the letter and get connected, then write me at www.EncourageMentors.info and stay connected. My team created the website in the hope that readers who have been moved by these attitude steps would stay in touch. Please share with me your letter or send me your favorite story of encouragement, your adventures in mentoring and being mentored. In addition, read the posts of others who have found encouragement in the likeliest and unlikeliest of places.

What better reason to get in touch and stay connected?

*JoAn's beautiful blended family*

*The blended family JoAn grew up with*

# ENCOURAGEMENTORS IN MY LIFE:
## (NOT MENTIONED IN THIS BOOK)

Ana Quillinan

Beckey Boldger

Cindy Cross

Cindy McCoy

Cyndi Zwerneman

Danise & George Johnson

Dawn Bowers

Dr. Andrew DeJong

Dr. Benjamin (Ben) Young

Dr. Carl Misch

Dr. Donald Morgan

Dr. Gary McDonald

Dr. Jerry & Mary Burd

Dr. Joe & Anna Ebeling

Dr. Joe & Mary Majors

Dr. Jose Cappelan

Dr. Kevin Devine

Dr. Mac Lee

Dr. Mark Setter

Dr. Michael Brown & the Hand Surgery Center in Houston

Dr. Peter Dawson

Dr. Randy Resnik

Dr. Ray & Suzan Hazen

Dr. Robert & Emily Marroquin

Dr. Sharon Moore

Guy & Martha Huffman

Heidi Cartegena

James L. (Jim) Dunn, Sr.

James L. (Jim) Dunn, Jr.

Jeannie Price

Joe Lee Register

Julie Baker

Kathi Carlson

Kirpal Gordon

Marcy Norman

Michelle Gimbert

Miquette Uhrenholdt

Monetta Reyes

My nephew John Gonzalez &
all of the men and women in our
armed services whose strength
inspires me

My son's EncourageMentors at
school (you know who you are)

Pastor Steve Johnson

Pastor Todd Jordan

Rhonda Hadley

Sandy & David Porritt

Scott Sandel

Shirley Temple-Schmidt

Sue Dziobala

Susan Strand Wingrove

Vicki McManus

I am human and I am sure I have forgotten someone really special and important. Won't you please forgive me? I am sorry and wouldn't have hurt you on purpose. Me and deadlines... well that just about explains it all.

# BUY A SHARE OF THE FUTURE IN YOUR COMMUNITY

These certificates make great holiday, graduation and birthday gifts that can be personalized with the recipient's name. The cost of one S.H.A.R.E. or one square foot is $54.17. The personalized certificate is suitable for framing and will state the number of shares purchased and the amount of each share, as well as the recipient's name. The home that you participate in "building" will last for many years and will continue to grow in value.

**Here is a sample SHARE certificate:**

## YES, I WOULD LIKE TO HELP!

*I support the work that Habitat for Humanity does and I want to be part of the excitement! As a donor, I will receive periodic updates on your construction activities but, more importantly, I know my gift will help a family in our community realize the dream of homeownership.* **I would like to SHARE in your efforts against substandard housing in my community!** *(Please print below)*

PLEASE SEND ME _____ SHARES at $54.17 EACH = $ $_____

*In Honor Of:* _____

*Occasion: (Circle One)*    HOLIDAY    BIRTHDAY    ANNIVERSARY

      OTHER: _____

*Address of Recipient:* _____

*Gift From:* _____  *Donor Address:* _____

*Donor Email:* _____

**I AM ENCLOSING A CHECK FOR $ $_____ PAYABLE TO HABITAT FOR HUMANITY OR PLEASE CHARGE MY VISA OR MASTERCARD** *(CIRCLE ONE)*

Card Number _____ Expiration Date: _____

Name as it appears on Credit Card _____ Charge Amount $ _____

Signature _____

Billing Address _____

Telephone # Day _____ Eve _____

**PLEASE NOTE:** Your contribution is tax-deductible to the fullest extent allowed by law.
**Habitat for Humanity • P.O. Box 1443 • Newport News, VA 23601 • 757-596-5553**
**www.HelpHabitatforHumanity.org**

Printed in the USA
CPSIA information can be obtained
at www.ICGtesting.com
JSHW082222140824
68134JS00015B/681